The LITTLE BOOK of
Cut-flower
Gardening

RHS The Little Book of Cut-flower Gardening

Author: Holly Farrell

First published in Great Britain in 2023 by Mitchell Beazley, a division of
Octopus Publishing Group Ltd
Carmelite House, 50 Victoria Embankment, London EC4Y 0DZ
www.octopusbooks.co.uk
An Hachette UK Company
www.hachette.co.uk

Published in association with the Royal Horticultural Society

ISBN: 978-1-78472-889-2

A CIP record of this book is available from the British Library

Printed and bound in China

Conceived, designed and produced by The Bright Press
an imprint of The Quarto Group, 1 Triptych Place, London,
SE1 9SH, United Kingdom
T (0) 20 7700 6700
www.Quarto.com

Publisher: James Evans
Art Director: James Lawrence
Editorial Director: Isheeta Mustafi
Managing Editor: Jacqui Sayers
Editor: Emily Angus
Project Editor: Polly Goodman
Design and Image Research: Lindsey Johns
Illustrations: John Woodcock, Lindsey Johns
Mitchell Beazley Publisher: Alison Starling
Mitchell Beazley Editorial Assistant: Jeannie Stanley
RHS Publisher: Helen Griffin
RHS Consultant Editor: Simon Maughan
RHS Head of Editorial: Tom Howard

The Royal Horticultural Society is the UK's leading gardening charity dedicated to advancing
horticulture and promoting good gardening. Its charitable work includes providing expert advice
and information, training the next generation of gardeners, creating hands-on opportunities for
children to grow plants and conducting research into plants, pests and environmental issues
affecting gardeners.

For more information visit www.rhs.org.uk or call 0845 130 4646.

RHS

The LITTLE BOOK of

Cut-flower Gardening

HOW TO GROW FLOWERS AND FOLIAGE
SUSTAINABLY FOR BEAUTIFUL ARRANGEMENTS

HOLLY FARRELL

MITCHELL BEAZLEY

CONTENTS

INTRODUCTION

A vase of fresh flowers is a joyful thing. Flowers brighten our homes, our lives and, when they are home-grown, they also brighten our gardens, not just for us, but also for the buzzing wildlife that loves their nectar. Growing your own cut flowers gives the huge satisfaction of harvesting something from a plant you have nurtured, and brings a greater connection with nature and the seasons. It also allows you to have a house full of flowers all year round at a fraction of the cost of buying bouquets, all with a sustainable, positive, environmental impact.

Having a cut-flower patch means you can grow a huge variety of flowers that are simply not available in the shops. You might want to grow sweet peas like your granny did, roses that actually have some fragrance, or perhaps you'd just like a bit more choice for your weekly bunch of blooms. Whatever your reasons for wanting to start a cutting garden, you'll find that by growing your own, you'll be able to fill your home with many more flowers, different types of flowers, and have a beautiful garden to boot, all for the fraction of the cost of the bouquets you'd buy in the shops.

The worldwide cut-flower industry means that we can buy roses, lilies and more all year round; we have lost what it means to look forward to the first rose of summer and enjoy it all the more for its fleeting nature. Looking at flowers and having them in our homes makes us feel better – imagine how good you'll feel when you know you grew those flowers yourself, that you helped support the birds, bees and butterflies as you did so, and that your flowers are connecting you back to the wild, to Mother Nature and to her cycle of the year.

Left Grow your own roses to enjoy their beautiful scent, which is so often lacking from shop-bought blooms.

HOW TO USE THIS BOOK

Whatever your experience as a gardener and whatever your knowledge of flowers, this book offers a complete guide to growing, cutting and arranging your own flowers, including buying seeds and plants.

CHAPTER 1:
A YEAR OF FLOWERS
Introduces the possibilities for your cutting patch, and how to plan to make the most of the space and time you have for growing flowers.

CHAPTER 2:
GROWING FLOWERS
Contains all the practical and general information you need to start growing flowers, from the tools you'll need, to how to sow and save seeds, look after your soil, and how to dry flowers.

CHAPTER 3: PLANT PROFILES

Consists of profiles of different flowering plants that you might like to grow. These are divided into how they grow – whether they are annuals or perennials – and then subdivided into further sections (such as shrubs for foliage, roses, grasses, and winter stems and berries) to make it easy for you to choose what to plant on your patch.

Each profile has a set of at-a-glance information – how tall and wide the plant will get, when it flowers, the range of colours the different varieties of the plant can supply and how long it should last in the vase. There are also specifics of growing each plant that should be taken in conjunction with the general advice in Chapter 2; suggestions of varieties of that flower that you might like as well as the one in the heading; and occasionally some different plants that will give you a similar effect.

Finally, the book ends with a glossary explaining technical terms and how plant names work, and a resources section including seed retailers, websites, books and other inspirational sources that will help you get going with growing cut flowers.

CHAPTER ONE

A Year of Flowers

A cutting garden is a beautiful space, filled with flowers, bees and butterflies. However, cutting gardens work best when they are designed as a utilitarian space, a productive plot of cut-flower crops. This view may seem harsh, but it is exactly this approach that makes a successful cut-flower patch, because it means you can cut the flowers without any lingering guilt that it will have a detrimental effect on your garden. The flowers you grow are destined for your kitchen table, desk, hallway or bedside table, or to be given away to friends and family, and it is there that you will enjoy and cherish them all the more for knowing that you raised and nurtured them yourself.

Of course, you will enjoy spending time in your cutting patch and the process of tending it, no matter how big or small it is, but by having a separate patch specifically for cutting flowers, you can grow them like crops, making the most of the space and your time with some careful planning and efficiencies.

PLANNING YOUR CUTTING PATCH

No matter the size of your garden or allotment, when starting a cutting patch it pays to begin in a small way. Growing your own flowers is hugely enjoyable, but best practice is to keep your plans realistic so the patch doesn't become overwhelming. You can then build on your successes each year, gradually increasing your plot size or variety if you like.

WHAT DO YOU WANT TO GROW?

Spend some time with Chapter 3 of this book thinking about your favourite flowers and the style of your home. Do you want to fill it with blowsy, vintage jugs of a variety of blooms, or have sleek, glass vases of just one variety? Which flower fragrances do you love? The answers to these questions will inform what you want to grow, and how much of it.

WHAT CAN YOU GROW?

Annual plants flower within a few months and are some of the easiest with which to start a cutting patch. Annuals are grown from seed, making them relatively inexpensive per plant, and are often cut-and-come again (see pp14–15), giving you lots of flowers per plant. Biennial plants are sown in the summer of one year and flower the following spring.

Perennial plants that are useful for cut flowers include woody shrubs such as hydrangeas, and herbaceous perennials such as phlox and delphiniums, whose stems and foliage die back for winter but shoot anew in spring. Perennials are less labour-intensive than annuals and biennials, but they are a bigger initial investment in either money (if you buy them as plants) or patience (if you sow them as seeds, as they will take a year or two to bulk up to cutting size). Climbers are good for trailing out of the vase and make use of the vertical space in the garden, and you may also want some evergreens or colourful stems for winter interest and wreath-making.

Opposite Dahlias are stalwarts of the cutting patch, and are available in many different colours and forms, including these elegant, daisy-type flowers.

GETTING THE MOST FROM YOUR PATCH

A little careful planning beforehand can help you to get the most from your space. By using different types of plants that bloom in succession, you can be cutting flowers from spring to autumn. Thinking about how to maximise the efficiency of your patch might not be the most romantic aspect of cut-flower growing, but it's worth it when you're gathering armfuls of flowers all season long.

CUT-AND-COME-AGAIN BLOOMS

By far the easiest and most economical way to produce a lot of flowers is to grow plants that continue to produce more blooms after you've cut the first flush; these are known as 'cut-and-come-again' plants and will form the backbone of your cutting patch. Flower growers take advantage of plants' biological imperative to produce seeds by cutting the flowers the plant continues to produce in the hope that it will be able to set seed before the autumn.

Cut-and-come-again annuals, such as sweet peas, cosmos and cornflowers, can produce flowers for many months if they are cut regularly. Other plants that produce more than one set of flowers include perennials such as dahlias and repeat-flowering roses. Again, these are the real workhorses of the cutting patch, needing less input than the single-flowering plants relative to their output.

Left Snapdragons are a traditional cottage-garden favourite that make an excellent cut flower.

Right Cut-and-come-again dahlias, like these ball-type flowers, continue to supply their big, beautiful blooms all through late summer and early autumn.

SINGLE BLOOMS

Some plants, such as sunflowers and foxgloves, which are ostensibly single-blooming, can also produce more than one harvest. After their main flower stem has been cut, these plants will often produce branches of secondary, smaller flowers.

PLANT VARIETY FOR A LONG PICKING PERIOD

Growing a variety of annuals, biennials, bulbs and perennials means you can have something to pick from early spring to late autumn, and even through the winter. Spring bulbs and blossom will be the first harvest, followed by biennials and early perennials, then annuals and more bulbs and perennials in summer, with the season closing with half-hardy annuals, perennial flowers and grasses in autumn. In winter, evergreen foliage and winter-flowering shrubs come to the fore, and if you've dried flowers and seedheads of your summer crops, these will also provide colour and interest in the colder months.

Below Nothing heralds late spring like a vase full of sprightly tulips.

MAKING THE BEST USE OF YOUR SPACE

A healthy, well-looked-after soil will produce a more bountiful harvest and support several crops through the growing season (see also pp44–9). Plants can be layered and planted in succession to take full advantage of the space you have available. Plant bulbs between rows of perennials (their foliage will have died down by the time the perennials get going in summer), or sow or plant annuals in late spring between the bulbs, to get a double harvest from a single area.

Above You could also plant bulbs for cutting in your flower borders, to make the most use of the space in your garden.

Making successional sowings, and having a growing space (such as a sunny windowsill or greenhouse) where you can raise plants from seed in small pots before planting them out, means one harvest is more quickly replaced by another. For example, your annual marigold and love-in-a-mist seedlings can be happily growing in pots while you're still cutting biennials, ready to plant out once the spring flowers have finished. The annuals will start flowering soon after, but if you'd waited to sow them direct into the ground after removing the biennials, your first cuttings would not be for several weeks.

GROWING IN CONTAINERS AND UNDER COVER

You don't need a garden or allotment to grow your own cut flowers. If you've space for a few pots, you can be raising plants and cutting fresh blooms for your home. If you do have the space (and, potentially, the budget) for a greenhouse, it can be a useful addition to your cutting patch, but it's far from essential.

GROWING IN POTS

Use the biggest containers you can, and layer the planting to maximise the space as you would for plants in the ground (see p17). Fill them with home-made or peat-free, multi-purpose compost, water regularly and give them a liquid feed every week or fortnight (see p49). Pots are also useful for permanent plantings of tender plants as they can be moved to a sheltered spot for winter.

Above Pots can be useful to grow flowers that wouldn't thrive in your flower patch; in a plot with wet winter soil these agapanthus can be given the well-drained conditions they prefer in a pot.

GROWING IN RAISED BEDS

Putting raised beds over hard surfaces, in a courtyard for example, can be more economical in the long term and is certainly easier to maintain than the equivalent-sized cutting patch in individual pots. Raised beds can hold more water (so less time for you with the watering can); you're able to plant in rows, making maintenance more straightforward; and you can keep mulching the top rather than having to replace compost in pots each year (see also p49). Construct your raised beds of any sustainably sourced timber (repurposed or recycled if possible), making them at least 30cm (1ft) deep.

GROWING UNDER COVER

If you have the space and budget for one, a greenhouse can be handy. Keep an eye on local ads – you can sometimes get lucky and see one going free if you are able to dismantle and remove it yourself.

GREENHOUSES

Greenhouses are useful for raising early sown seedlings in spring; over-wintering, autumn-sown plants; growing flowers to maturity protected from the weather; bleaching dried flowers; storing dahlia tubers over winter; and bringing on pots of bulbs or annuals earlier in spring.

SEASONAL TASKS

The rise and fall of the gardening year, from the intensity of the new spring growth to the hazy days of summer harvests and the gradual senescence of autumn and drawing in of winter, is a rhythm that it's easy to reconnect with through gardening. Each time of year brings new joys, like reuniting with old friends; the more you garden, the more you'll become familiar with and look forward to the season's tasks.

SPRING

- Start cutting bulbs and biennial flowers.

- Sow annuals under cover in pots in early spring; plant out in late spring.

- Remove weeds and rake/ prepare the soil for sowing.

- Sow annuals direct from mid-spring once the soil is warm.

- Pot up dahlia tubers.

- Put in plant supports.

- Water in dry and windy spells.

SUMMER

- Harvest your flowers regularly, especially cut-and-come-again varieties.

- Water in dry spells.

- Regularly water and give a liquid feed to container-grown plants.

- Plant out dahlias and half-hardy annuals in early summer, after the last frost.

- Order bulbs for autumn planting.

- Sow biennials.

AUTUMN

- Continue harvesting flowers, grasses and seedheads.

- Plant perennials, trees and shrubs.

- Plant bulbs.

- Plant out pot-sown biennials.

- Save seed.

- Clear away and compost annuals that have died back.

- Sow green manures on bare soil.

- Prune roses in late autumn early winter.

- Make leaf mould.

WINTER

- Decide what to grow next year and order seeds.

- Tidy up your patch in late winter, cutting back perennials and green manures.

- Apply a mulch of organic matter.

- Clean your pots and tools.

- Harvest festive evergreens and winter-flowering shrubs.

Right Pruning roses in late autumn promotes fresh growth and branching, giving you more flowers for cutting.

SOWING, PLANTING AND FLOWERING CALENDAR

Sow ·············
Plant ════════
Flower ────────

Whether you'd like to grow enough for a posy every week from early spring to late autumn, or you need to fill a hall with flowers in June for a wedding, this quick reference guide will show you approximately when all of the flowering plants listed in Chapter 3 will bloom, and when you'll need to sow or plant them. Note that the flowering period highlighted is how long that plant should be in flower, not necessarily how long you can be picking for, as not all plants will repeat flower after a harvest.

	JAN	FEB	MAR	APR	MAY	JUNE	JULY	AUG	SEPT	OCT	NOV	DEC
Sweet peas	Sow	Sow	Sow		Flower	Flower	Flower	Flower	Flower	Sow	Sow	
Cornflower		Sow	Sow	Sow	Flower	Flower						
Love-in-a-mist		Sow	Sow	Sow	Flower		Flower	Flower		Sow	Sow	
White laceflower		Sow	Sow	Sow	Sow		Flower	Flower				
Toothpick plant		Sow	Sow	Sow			Flower	Flower				
Common marigold		Sow	Sow	Sow			Flower	Flower		Sow	Sow	
Sunflower				Sow	Sow		Flower					
Poppy				Sow	Sow			Flower	Flower			
Fiddleneck		Sow	Sow	Sow		Flower	Flower		Flower			
Honeywort	Sow	Sow	Sow	Sow		Flower	Flower		Flower			
Branching larkspur			Sow	Sow	Sow		Flower	Flower		Flower		
Cosmos				Sow	Sow			Flower	Flower			
Tobacco plant		Sow	Sow	Sow	Sow							
Snapdragon	Sow	Sow	Sow	Sow			Flower	Flower	Flower	Flower		
Blue lace flower			Sow				Flower	Flower				
Love-lies-bleeding			Sow	Sow			Flower	Flower				
Spider flower	Sow	Sow	Sow	Sow				Flower	Flower			
Zinnia			Sow	Sow	Sow				Flower	Flower		
Mexican paintbrush	Sow	Sow	Sow	Sow		Flower	Flower	Flower	Flower			
Foxglove				Plant	Plant							
Honesty					Flower	Flower	Flower					
Stocks						Plant	Plant					
Wild carrot	Sow	Sow	Sow			Flower	Flower	Flower			Sow	Sow
Iceland poppy						Plant	Plant					
Wallflower			Flower	Flower	Flower		Plant	Plant				

	JAN	FEB	MAR	APR	MAY	JUNE	JULY	AUG	SEPT	OCT	NOV	DEC
Hellebore	▬	▬	▬						░	░		
Masterwort			░		▬	▬	▬	▬	▬			
Lady's mantle			░			▬	▬	▬	▬	▬	▬	
Peony			░		▬				░	░		
Sneezeweed			░			▬	▬	▬	░	░		
Yarrow			░				▬	▬	░			
Penstemon			░			▬	▬	▬	▬	▬	▬	
Bergamot			░				▬	▬	░			
Peruvian lily				░	░	░	▬					
Chocolate cosmos			░	░			▬	▬				
Delphinium			░			▬			░	░		
African lily			░				▬	▬	▬	▬		
Perennial phlox			░				▬	▬				
Lavender			░				▬		░	░		
Michaelmas daisy			░					▬	░	░		
Sea holly			░				▬	▬	░			
Golden oats grass			░			▬	▬	▬	░	░		
Hare's tail grass			░				▬	▬	░	░		
Daffodil	▬	▬	░	▬					░	░		
Hyacinth		▬	▬						░	░		
Tulip			▬	▬	▬						░	
Persian buttercup					▬							
Lily of the valley					▬				░	░		
Allium						▬	▬		░	░		
Lily						▬	▬	▬	░			
Grassnut						▬			░	░		
Gladioli									░	░		
Dahlia					░	░		▬	░			
Rose		░	░			▬			░	░		
Cherry			░	▬	▬							
Winter-flowering honeysuckle		▬							░	░		
Hydrangea		░	░						░	░		
Mock orange		░				▬			░	░		
Honeysuckle		░			▬	▬	▬	▬	░	░		
Clematis		▬	░			▬	▬	▬	░	░		
Dogwood		░	░						░	░	▬	▬
Goat willow		░	░						░	░		

CHAPTER TWO

Growing Flowers

Growing your own flowers may bring you as much pleasure as looking at them once they are in the vase. Gardening is a joyful, meditative and calming activity, proven in numerous studies to have a positive effect both on mental wellbeing and physical health.

Having a bounteous cut-flower garden means you will also be benefitting the bees, butterflies and moths as well as the ladybirds, birds and other creatures that feed on the insects that your flowers will attract. By growing your flowers without pesticides and encouraging natural predators, your cut-flower patch could be a haven for wildlife, as well as providing floriferous harvests for you.

Both perennial and annual flowers are straightforward to grow and, by following the few basic principles set out in this chapter, you could be harvesting buckets of flowers within a few short months.

ORGANIC AND SUSTAINABLE APPROACHES

By growing your own cut flowers, you can avoid supporting and perpetuating the negative environmental effects that are characteristic of many imported, shop-bought flowers. Growing your own flowers means you can have a positive impact on the environment; help wildlife and – because they don't have to travel to get to you – your blooms will have zero 'flower miles'.

GROWING METHODS

Organic growers do not use any pesticides, herbicides or other artificial substances on their gardens. Like permaculture gardeners, they aim to create a healthy and balanced ecosystem in which they tolerate minor damage by insects or slugs because these creatures are food for birds, toads and hedgehogs.

Creating a balanced ecosystem in your cutting patch will encourage natural predators of undesirable insects: for example, hoverflies and ladybirds (and their larvae) will feast on aphids.

REDUCING PLASTIC

Make your own biodegradable small pots from the individual sections of old egg boxes, or from newspaper using a paper pot maker.

Vegan gardeners avoid any animal-derived substances, such as blood, fish and bone fertilizer. Biodynamic gardeners follow timetables for sowing and planting based on the phases of the moon, as well as certain recipes for fertilizers.

All these growing styles have the same underlying principle that looking after the soil is the foundation of good gardening. You may choose to follow one discipline, or cherry-pick from several, but the main thing is to grow in a way that best suits you, and the time and budget you have available for your patch.

ENVIRONMENTALLY FRIENDLY GARDENING

Whilst gardening in general has a positive environmental effect, there are some aspects of the horticultural industry that are harmful to wildlife, and also use petrochemicals and plastic heavily. To garden your cut-flower patch in the most environmentally friendly way, avoid plastic and any single-use items wherever possible. Rather than buying compost in plastic sacks, buy in bulk (share a load with neighbours) or buy loose in a refillable bag, or make your own. Always buy peat-free compost, to avoid depleting peat bogs that are carbon sinks and invaluable wildlife habitats. Try to buy plants in non-plastic pots or bare root. Reuse any plastic pots and sacks you do acquire until they fall apart, then recycle them at garden centres and supermarkets.

TOOLS AND EQUIPMENT

Depending on the size of your patch, it's possible to improvise with many garden tools, avoiding a big outlay on equipment at the beginning. See if your local town has a tools library, or if you can borrow from friends and neighbours until you are sure you need a particular tool of your own. Most garden tools can last a lifetime when properly cared for with regular cleaning and sharpening, so when buying tools, invest in the best quality available within your budget. Good-quality second-hand tools are a great option too and can be sourced online, at boot fairs and second-hand shops, or from specialist suppliers of reconditioned old tools.

BASIC KIT

TROWEL for digging planting holes and scooping compost.

RAKE for levelling the soil and removing stones before sowing seeds.

GARDEN FORK for turning compost into the soil and turning the compost heap.

SPADE for digging planting holes for larger plants.

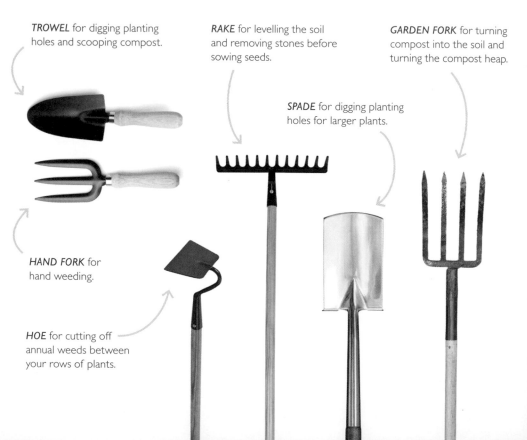

HAND FORK for hand weeding.

HOE for cutting off annual weeds between your rows of plants.

CANES OR STAKES for supporting tall and climbing plants, and newly planted trees.

GARDEN TWINE for climbing and tall plants, and creating netting supports. Biodegradable twine can be composted, saving detaching it from old plants in autumn.

PLANT LABELS to identify sowing dates and variety names, ideally non-plastic, reuseable ones.

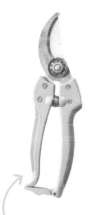

WATERING CAN with a detachable rose attachment for the spout.

FLORISTRY SCISSORS for cutting your flowers, although normal kitchen scissors will do.

SMALL POTS, WATERPROOF TRAYS AND COMPOST in which to raise young plants from seed (see also pp32–4).

PAIR OF SECATEURS for cutting back and pruning. For non-woody plants, a strong pair of scissors will suffice at first.

TRUGS, BASKETS OR BUCKETS for gathering your flowers once cut. Second-hand metal buckets and wooden or wicker trugs and baskets have a vintage feel and are better choices environmentally.

GET GROWING: SEEDS OR PLANTS?

There are various ways to get your cutting patch started, depending on what works for you, your space and your budget. The main options for buying plants, each with their own considerations, are growing from seed, young plants in trays ('plug plants'), or from larger potted plants.

GROWING FLOWERS FROM SEED

There is a far greater choice of varieties to buy as seed than there is as plants. Seed is also relatively inexpensive, can give you many plants from a single packet, and is more sustainable, too – the packets are small and recyclable, the shipping costs to the environment are lower than moving plants around, and you can then sow them in the compost of your choice rather than that of the retailers. Once your patch is up and running, it's even cheaper and more sustainable to save your own seed (see pp64–5).

However, you might have germination problems, or lose seedlings to pests or the weather. If you sow into small pots before planting out to avoid these problems, you'll need space in which to do so, such as a greenhouse or sunny windowsill. Furthermore, some cut-flower plants can't be grown from seed, and some perennials grown from seed will take a few years before they are big enough to start cutting.

GROWING FLOWERS FROM PLANTS

For roses, trees, shrubs and some perennials, it's worth investing in potted plants (though see if friends and neighbours have some that you can divide or take cuttings from first). Some may be available 'bare root' in the autumn and winter, which are generally less expensive than their potted equivalents. Annual cut flowers can also be bought as plug plants. These are useful if you've lost your own seedlings, missed sowing windows, or want to get off to a quick start. However, there is less choice of variety and they are relatively expensive both in monetary and environmental terms.

TIPS FOR BUYING SEEDS AND PLANTS

Always tip the plant out of its pot to check the roots are healthy and not rootbound. The foliage should be strong, green and healthy-looking, with no pests or diseases (check under the leaves, too). When buying online, ensure your retailer has a no-quibbles return policy. Ensure seeds are well within the 'sow-by' date printed on the packet.

TOP-FIVE CUT FLOWERS FOR NOVICE GARDENERS

Hardy annual flowers are the most straightforward to grow and require little initial outlay. These five will grow reliably from seed in most gardens, and give you plenty of cut-and-come-again flowers from spring to autumn.

Cornflower
Hardy plants keep producing their frilly blue, button-head flowers all summer long, and they're easy to save seed from, too.

Sunflower
Grow the smaller, branching varieties – they'll give you more blooms and won't be top-heavy in the vase.

Common marigold
For cheerful, orange and yellow flowers, this garden stalwart is hard to beat, flowering from spring to autumn.

Fiddleneck
These pretty flowers will also attract bees and butterflies to your plot, and the foliage helps suppress weeds.

Sweet pea
A wigwam of scented sweet peas can be fitted into a large pot or grown in the ground, giving a lot of flowers from a small space.

TOP-FIVE CUT FLOWERS FOR WEDDINGS

Which flowers to grow for a wedding depends considerably on the wedding's date — which influences what will be available — and the weather, which can make or break even the best-laid plans. Growing repeat-flowering annuals or perennials is the safest bet, and don't forget filler and foliage plants for fragrance and froth.

Rose
The ultimate flower of romance, and useful at any stage from in bud to full bloom. Don't forget to shave off any thorns before tying stems in a bouquet.

Dahlia
For later-season nuptials, cut-and-come-again dahlias are a must, and they're available in shades and forms to suit any colour scheme.

Cosmos
The daisy-like, pure-white cosmos add a delicate, meadow feel to a bouquet, perfect for the wilder wedding.

Toothpick plant
These big, frothy flower heads will fill out an arrangement quickly, and they're sculptural in bud and in flower.

Herbs
Fragrant foliage such as mint, lemon balm, bay and oregano add greenery and scent that will last the whole day.

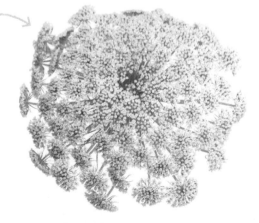

SOWING AND PLANTING

Most seeds are sown in mid-spring, although some biennials can be sown in midsummer or autumn. Perennials, trees and shrubs are best planted in the autumn, when the soil is still warm and there is relatively reliable rain to water them. This gives them time to establish, ready to grow strongly the following spring. Bare root plants can be put in the ground until spring provided the soil is not frozen or waterlogged.

SOWING SEEDS IN POTS

If you've space, either on a sunny windowsill or in a greenhouse, it can be useful to sow some of your seeds in small pots before planting out as young plants. Half-hardy annuals and perennials grown from seed are best raised in this way. Starting a portion of your hardy annual seeds in small pots a few weeks ahead of your direct sowings both hedges your losses (to the weather or slugs) and extends your harvesting time.

Your small pots should be around 5–10cm (2–4in) in diameter and on a watertight tray. Fill the pots with peat-free, multipurpose, sieved, home-made or seed compost and water thoroughly. Sow two seeds per pot. Water if the compost dries out using a rose attachment or by adding water to the tray.

Your seedlings will be ready to plant out when they are a good size and their roots have developed into all of the compost of the pot, but before they are rootbound. However, it will help if you harden them off for a week or so first by putting them outside in the daytime for around five days. For the next couple of days leave them out overnight as well, but covered with an upturned box. Only plant out half-hardy or frost-tender plants once all risk of frost has passed.

Use the plant profiles in Chapter 3 and the calendar on pp22–23 for specific information on when to sow, plant (and cut) each flower.

SOWING SEEDS IN THE SOIL

Sowing seeds straight into the soil, raised bed or large container where they are to grow as plants is known as direct sowing. Ensure the area is weed-free, stone free and raked level, water it thoroughly and then scrape out a shallow trench. Sprinkle your seeds sparingly along this trench, cover back over and pat down the soil. Alternatively, make individual holes along the row, spaced accordingly, and drop in two seeds before covering over, known as station sowing. Label with the date and the plant name.

PLANTING BULBS IN THE SOIL

Bulbs that will be left in the soil for many seasons can be planted, pointed end upwards, in the same way as station-sowing. If they are to be lifted and replanted elsewhere, or discarded after their flowering season, they can be planted in a trench almost touching each other.

SOWING SEEDS

As a general rule, bury seeds and bulbs in a hole or trench twice the depth of their size. Very small seeds should be sprinkled on the surface and covered with a thin layer of compost. Always water the compost or soil before sowing to avoid washing the seeds away or into uneven clumps.

Left Grow a succession of blooms in one pot by layering bulbs in a 'lasagne'. Put the biggest bulbs (such as tulips, hyacinths and daffodils) in the lower layers and the smallest (such as croci and muscari) uppermost.

PLANTING BULBS IN POTS

A layered bulb 'lasagne' maximizes the use of the space and allows for several harvests from one pot. Put at least 10cm (4in) of peat-free multipurpose compost in the base of a container and arrange the bulbs on top, pointy end up and about 5cm (2in) apart. The largest and latest flowering bulbs, such as tulips, should go on the base layer. Cover with a layer of compost, then repeat to add up to three more layers and a final covering, with the smallest bulbs, such as snowdrops or muscari, in the top layer. Water well and ensure the compost doesn't dry out over winter. After flowering, potted bulbs can be planted out into borders, replanted in a pot in fresh compost, or discarded onto the compost heap.

THINNING SEEDLINGS

Wait until the seedlings in the ground are a good size, then remove the weakest ones to leave healthy, stocky plants at the appropriate spacing for their species. Good spacing will help prevent plants becoming thin and leggy.

PLANTING YOUNG PLANTS

Ensure any individual supports are erected before planting. Dig a small hole with a trowel and carefully insert your young plant's rootball, then firm it in well by pushing the soil around it towards the plant. Don't press down around the base of the plant or you could damage the young roots and delicate stem. Water well. Young plants in biodegradable pots can be planted in their pot, but ensure the whole of the pot is buried below the surface or it can act as a wick, drawing moisture up and away from the roots.

PINCHING OUT

Plants will produce more flowers the more stems they have, so pinch out the tops of annuals to encourage branching when the plants are still seedlings. Once they have two sets of true leaves, pinch off the growing tip to just above the topmost/second set of leaves.

If you are potting on seedlings into a slightly larger pot, part-fill the pot with seed compost (or use sieved, home-made or multi-purpose, peat-free compost), then place the seedling. Hold it upright by a leaf, never the delicate stem, and fill in around the rootball with compost. Tap the base of the pot a few times to settle everything together, then water it. Top up the compost level afterwards if necessary.

Below Take the time to plant shrubs and trees well, so they will get off to a good start and reward you with many years of healthy growth and flowers.

PLANTING LARGER PLANTS AND TREES

Dig a hole as wide and as deep as the rootball of your plant and hammer in a stake for trees. Position the plant in the hole. Bare root plants should have the root flare at soil level. Water the hole thoroughly (a full can's worth), then hold the plant/tree upright as you backfill around the roots with soil, firming it in well afterwards with your hands or the heel of your boot. Fix trees to their stakes with a tree tie. Label the plants or make a note of the variety on a garden plan.

SUPPORTING THE PLANTS

Tall and climbing plants need stakes and support, so even if your site is not windy, it's worth putting in supports to avoid them being flattened by heavy downpours or gusts of wind. It's always easier to put in supports at the beginning of the growing season so the plants can grow up through them, rather than the fiddlier job of trying to stake mature plants. Hazel poles are more sustainable and attractive than bamboo canes – if you've space, grow your own, or source from local woodland suppliers.

STAKING AND SUPPORT OPTIONS

For medium or tall, non-climbing plants, the easiest method is to create a horizontal net of biodegradable twine zig-zagged between posts or stakes. Put in posts at each corner of your bed and along the sides depending on its size. Fix the twine at a height of around 45cm (18in), winding it all around the edge and across the middle of the bed in various directions to create a net-like structure. Alternatively, buy natural, jute netting and stretch it between the posts.

Climbers such as sweet peas and clematis can be grown up sturdy wigwams of poles or canes. Each pole should have a third of its length in the soil. Add some twiggy bits of the climbers around the base, or tie the plants in loosely to guide them up the wigwam. Shorter tee-pees can be made around individual rose and dahlia bushes to support their branches.

Flowers with one or more tall stems, such as sunflowers, foxgloves, delphiniums and cosmos, can be supported with individual stakes to which they are tied with garden twine.

Left Growing plants through jute netting (a more sustainable alternative to plastic) helps keep the flowers pristine and easy to cut.

Right A wigwam of hazel stakes looks attractive and can be used to support tall plants such as delphiniums.

CANE TOPPERS

Where you have stakes and posts that might be a hazard when you are bending to cut flowers and tend your plants, put cane toppers such as empty snail shells on them (paint them to make them more visible).

WATERING

Watering is straightforward, but it's important to get right. Overwatered plants will produce lots of lush foliage at the expense of flowers, but too little water can prompt early, smaller flowers with shorter stems. Using water, a limited resource, in a sustainable and effective way minimizes the effect on the wider environment, and is less wasteful of your time and resources.

REDUCING WATERING

Where possible, plant in the ground rather than containers as plants in the latter dry out faster. Plant perennials in the autumn if you can, and avoid planting in hot or windy weather at any time of year. Mulching around the base of plants with compost, leaf mould or even cardboard (see p49) can also help to reduce water loss from the soil.

Left A 'rose' on a watering-can spout will disperse the water more widely, helping to avoid washing away the compost, soil or young seedlings when watering.

WATER-SAVING TIPS

Ideally, install one or more water butts to catch and store rainwater. You can also use grey water on your flowers, but only do this every second or third watering to avoid soap building up in the soil. Using a watering can rather than a hosepipe makes you more mindful of how much water you are using

WHEN AND HOW TO WATER

Anything planted in a container will need regular checking and watering, including raised beds over the top of paving or concrete. Newly planted flowers and seedlings will need more watering than established plants, but in very dry or windy weather you may need to water most of your plants. Check the soil first – a dry crust can conceal damp soil beneath, and conversely light rain can dampen the surface but not penetrate to the roots. Dig a small hole in the soil around 20cm (8in) deep to check the moisture levels – if it's dry you will need to water.

Always give your plants a good soak rather than a quick splash, directing the water at the soil around the roots (not the leaves) and pausing between applications to allow it to sink in. Watering in the early morning rather than the middle of the day reduces water loss to evaporation. The evening is also better than midday, but leaves the soil damp overnight, which can encourage slugs and snails.

LOOKING AFTER THE SOIL

The soil is far more than an anchor for your plants' roots, it is a rich ecosystem full of life. Keeping it in tip-top condition doesn't just make for healthier plants and better flowers, it will also lock up carbon and help wildlife – the bugs and microbes that live in the soil are the basis of many animal food chains.

A HEALTHY SOIL

What kind of soil do you have – is it sandy, or does it press into clay-like lumps? Ideally it will be somewhere in between and resemble crumbled chocolate cake, with drainage that isn't too fast or slow.

SOIL pH

Measure your soil's acidity level (pH) with a home testing kit before you start. Most plants grow best in a neutral soil (pH 6.5-8), so if your pH is higher or lower than this, consider putting a shallow, raised bed over the top of the soil and filling it with bought-in topsoil and organic matter.

But all soils benefit enormously from the regular addition of organic matter (see p49) which, amongst other things, improves the soil structure and replaces nutrients the plants have used.

Spread a layer of organic matter around 10cm (4in) thick over the soil surface in late winter (called 'mulching'), at least a month before planting new plants or sowing seeds. Make sure it doesn't touch the stems of existing plants or they can rot.

Below Tending your cut flower beds little and often is less onerous than doing it all at once, and you can more easily spot and remove unwanted plants before they set seed.

CROP ROTATION

Rotating plants – not growing the same plant in the same spot each year – means you are less likely to get a build-up of harmful organisms in the soil that damage that plant. Rotating also helps keeps the soil nutrients balanced, as each species uses a slightly different nutrient range.

WEEDING

Unwanted plants can steal water, light and nutrients from your flowers. Removing them little and often, before they flower and set seed, is the easiest way to keep them under control. Learn to recognize the seedlings of flowers that might have self-seeded in your patch and you'll be able to transplant them for new crops.

COMPOST AND COMPOSTING

Making your own compost keeps your cut flower patch a closed loop of nutrient recycling: all the plant material you remove (and the spent cut flowers) can all be rotted down into a rich, crumbly fertilizer and soil improver to add back to the garden.

WHAT IS COMPOST AND ORGANIC MATTER?

'Compost' can mean both the growing medium sold in bags and the well-rotted product of your own compost heap. 'Organic matter' is any rotted plant or animal material – it has a natural origin, but is not necessarily free from artificial chemicals such as herbicides. Good types of organic matter are compost, well-rotted manure or leaf mould (composted leaves).

Note that bought compost should be used as soon as possible, so check the sell-by date on the bag before you buy.

MAKING COMPOST

A healthy compost heap will be a roughly equal balance of green/wet and brown/dry material. 'Greens' include fresh plant material, grass clippings, weeds and vegetable peelings. Good 'browns' include thin, woody prunings, paper and

cardboard, dry plant stalks and leaves, cut up old clothes (only 100% cotton or wool), human and pet hair, and wood shavings such as hamster bedding.

Don't add cooked food waste, oils and fats, meat, fish or dairy products, or cat or dog poo (although some specialist composting systems can cope with these items). The roots of pernicious, perennial weeds such as horsetail and bindweed should be killed before adding to compost heaps. Either dry them out completely or soak them in water for a month. All styles of compost heap benefit from regular turning to incorporate air (be careful of toads and slow worms hiding within it), which helps it to rot efficiently – if it smells, it's too wet and doesn't have enough air, so add lots of browns and turn it.

MAKING LEAF MOULD

Simply bag up fallen tree and shrub leaves in the autumn in hessian or old plastic compost sacks (punch some air holes in the sides if the latter). Water the leaves if they're dry, tie up the top and leave for one to two years to rot down.

Below The bigger your cut-flower patch, the more composting capacity you will need. Ensure your bins are easy to access, to remove the compost when it's ready.

RAISING HEALTHY PLANTS

Healthy plants produce the best flowers. Your plants will need plenty of light, water and a good soil that supplies them with a balance of nutrients. Feeding the soil is more important than feeding the plants; a healthy soil will feed the plants in turn. It is possible to grow cut flowers closer together than border flowers because the act of cutting reduces their overall size, but don't be tempted to cram in too many.

SPACE TO GROW

Plants that are too tightly packed will grow tall and straggly, not sturdy and branching. Giving plants enough space also means better air circulation (reducing the likelihood of fungal diseases), and easier picking. Refer to Chapter 3 for the flower's height and spread, and allow enough distance between each plant (for plants of different species, take an average of their spreads).

Below Tulips can be planted very close together, but only if you are moving them elsewhere after they've finished flowering.

FEEDING THE SOIL AND PLANTS

Regular mulching is the simplest and most effective way to feed your soil. If your beds are going to be empty for a while, consider planting a green manure crop. There is a choice of types – some legumes, such as beans (e.g. *Vicia sativa*), and clover (*Trifolium*) will also help to add nitrogen into the soil, but all prevent the soil eroding in windy or wet weather, prevent weeds germinating, and provide shelter and food for beneficial insects.

A month before you want to plant the bed with flowers again, cut down the tops, chop up and allow to wilt, then turn them into the soil.

FERTILIZERS

Liquid fertilizers are a useful extra boost to plants through the growing season, and are especially needed by potted plants, which will exhaust the nutrients in their compost after about six weeks. Buy a proprietary (organic) seaweed fertilizer or make your own feed.

HOMEMADE PLANT FEED

Steeping a bucketful of nettle or comfrey leaves in water for around a month (cover the bucket to protect wildlife and your nose!) creates a 'tea' that can be watered onto plants undiluted. Put the steeped leaves into the compost or apply as a mulch. If you want to grow comfrey (*Symphytum officinale*), choose the sterile variety 'Bocking 14', which will flower but not self-seed all over your garden.

Right Cutting or tearing up your comfrey (or nettle) leaves to make 'tea' means that the nutrients they contain will more readily diffuse into the water.

WORKING WITH WILDLIFE

Your cutting patch will not just be vibrant with colourful flowers, it will also be bursting with wildlife, especially if you look after the soil. Insects, bugs, birds and if you're lucky frogs, hedgehogs and bats will use it for food and shelter. Working with the natural order is not only better for the planet but also more gratifying as a gardener. For the pleasure of watching a mob of long tailed tits, or butterflies resting on flowers, it's worth tolerating any damage they may cause.

WORKING WITH NATURE

A wildlife-friendly flower patch will encourage natural predators of creatures that may harm your crops. For example, blue tits and ladybirds will gobble up aphids, and wasps eat caterpillars – although you do need to be patient as there can be a lag between the problem becoming apparent and the predators moving in. This lag will decrease the more your plot becomes home to a diverse range of wildlife over the years. Working with nature within a thriving garden ecosystem is far preferable for you, wildlife and the wider environment than reaching for chemical pesticides, most of which kill indiscriminately and do much more harm than good.

For precious flower crops you could consider growing under cover of a greenhouse, but try to avoid netting, in which many animals can get fatally trapped, and plastic fleece and mesh products. Alternatively, regularly removing and rehoming problem creatures such as slugs can also help, but bear in mind if you remove the prey, you won't get the predators moving in.

BUILDING ECOSYSTEMS

Creating a flower patch will in itself attract all manner of pollinators and other insects, and the creatures that feed on them. Consider adding a hedgerow of trees and shrubs, which will provide food and shelter for many species of wildlife and be a windbreak for your cutting patch. A pond can also attract a wide range of insects and animals, including slug-eating toads, and that deadly insect predator, the dragonfly. Adding bird feeders to keep birds visiting your plot regularly and bug hotels for winter shelter will also help.

Opposite Creating homes and food for wildlife in your garden can bring you enormous joy, as well as supplying your patch with pollinators and useful predators.

WHEN AND HOW TO PICK

The perfect cutting time between budding and blooming depends on the species, so refer to Chapter 3 for more specific information. However, there are some general rules it's worth bearing in mind when cutting your flowers. This is the moment when all your patient nurturing of the plants starts to bear fruit, so take a moment to enjoy the act of harvesting itself.

WHAT YOU'LL NEED

- Scissors (floristry or kitchen) for cutting soft stems

- Secateurs for cutting woody stems

- A bucket one-quarter full of water

GOOD HYGIENE

Clean scissors/secateurs and buckets between harvests with soap and hot water, and if any plants are diseased (e.g. with mildew) you'll need to clean your cutting tools and hands with hand sanitiser before moving on to the next plants.

WHEN TO CUT

Cut at the coolest times of day if you can, ideally in the early morning but late evening is also fine, as this is when the flowers will be more fully hydrated. It's also better to cut in dry weather, as if the flowers are too soggy they may rot in the vase. Gently shake flowers to dislodge dew drops.

As soon as you have cut the stems, get them into the bucket of water. This is to prevent the spongy, water-transport tissue within the stems drying out – if they do, the flowers can struggle to rehydrate once they're in the vase. Woody stems also need cutting vertically up the stems a few centimetres (an inch), splitting them in half at their base to help create the maximum surface area for water absorption.

Above Put your flowers straight into a bucket of water after cutting. Daffodils benefit from changing the water (see p114).

Far left Support large blooms such as these dahlias while you cut the stem.

HOW TO CUT
. . . .

Make a clean cut just above a leaf or the point where the flower stalk branches from the main stem; if the cut is ragged, your tools need sharpening. Cut stems at an angle; this increases the surface area and ensures it will not sit flat on the vase base, both of which help the flower to take up water. Take as much stem for each bloom as possible, but leaving plenty of plant behind to branch and flower anew.

PREPARING THE FLOWERS

Home-grown cut flowers are as fresh as fresh can be when you arrange them in a vase, so most will last a week or more with no need for the chemical treatments the industry uses. You can arrange your flowers straight into their vase after picking, but they will look better and last longer if you allow time to condition and prepare them first.

PREPARING THE FLOWERS

Ideally, leave the cut stems in water for at least four hours before arranging them, preferably overnight. A cool, dark and well-ventilated place is best and the water should be just under the height of the shortest flowers. Any small, black pollen beetles will fly off towards the light, but you may need to gently wash off aphids.

To arrange, snip off the lower leaves so there is no foliage below the waterline in the vase. Recut the bottom of the stems at an angle (again also cutting vertically up woody stems).

SEARING

Home-grown flowers will not need searing as a rule, but it can be useful to revive stems that have wilted during conditioning.

Sear the conditioned and prepared stems by dipping the bottom few centimetres (one inch) of stem in a cup of boiling water for 20–30 seconds, protecting the bloom from the steam. Arrange straight into the vase.

Below Cut stems on a diagonal and to an appropriate length for the size of your vase.

EXTENDING VASE LIFE

Bacteria in the water are the enemy of cut flowers, so keep vases clean by washing them thoroughly in hot, soapy water between uses.

Keep your arrangements away from fruit or vegetables: as they ripen they release ethylene gas which will hasten the demise of your flowers.

To refresh an arrangement after a few days, change the water and recut the stems, removing a short length off the end. Replace any flowers that have gone over with fresh stems.

ARRANGING FLOWERS

How you arrange your flowers is entirely a matter of personal taste. The more you practise, the more skilled you will become in the art of choosing the right vase and arranging the flowers within it.

DESIGN BASICS

Simple, natural arrangements are often the most charming. Group your flowers according to their relative colours, but also consider their scents – they should not compete against each other, nor should an arrangement be olfactorily overwhelming. Put the foliage and fillers in the vase first, then add the flowers in odd numbers of single stems, or small groups.

Make your arrangement appropriately tall and wide for the space it will have. Cut your stems to different heights and put the tallest in the middle (and at the back, if it won't be viewed from behind).

Below Single flowers from one plant make an effective display in a group of smaller vases of the same ilk.

VASES AND MORE

The only crucial consideration for a vase
or other container is that it is watertight,
so keep an eye out for interesting vessels
for displaying your flowers, or repurpose
glass bottles or tins. You'll need a collection
of a few different sizes and styles, such as
smaller bottles or jam jars for sweet peas,
and larger vases and jugs for frothy or tall
displays such as ammi or sunflowers. If the
vase is too big or too small for the height
of the flowers, it can detract from the
overall effect.

SUPPORTING FLOWERS

Adding in some twiggy, woody stems
can help to hold up the floppier ones, or
tie the bunch together before putting it in
the vase. A smaller vase hidden within a
larger one can also help keep taller stems
upright, or use one with a narrower
neck (jugs are a good choice).

Florist's foam, or 'oasis', is now being
replaced with more environmentally
friendly options that are compostable
(oasis is plastic, and will not biodegrade).
An alternative for wider vases and bowls
is a ball of scrunched-up chicken wire
in the base into which the stems are
inserted, or get a reusable 'flower frog',
a ceramic, metal or glass mound with
stem-sized holes in it.

FLOWERS BY COLOUR

It can often be useful to plan your cutting patch around a particular colour palette – especially if you are growing for a particular event such as a wedding. Even for everyday arrangements, by growing flowers that all complement each other you can be sure of always being able to create a bouquet or posy with the flowers that you have, no matter what is blooming on that particular day. The lists below will give you a good start, but are by no means exhaustive.

Greens

Toothpick plant 'Green Mist'

Tobacco plant 'Lime Green'

Love-lies-bleeding 'Viridis'

Zinnia

Hellebore

Lady's mantle

Foliage herbs

Tulip

Hydrangea

Dogwood

Pinks and pastels

Yarrow

Fiddleneck

Cosmos

Mexican paintbrush

Foxglove

Honesty

Stocks

Peony

Hyacinth

Rose

Blues and whites

Sweet pea	White laceflower
Cornflower	Cosmos
Love-in-a-mist	Agapanthus
Branching larkspur	Lily of the valley
Poppy (fresh seedheads)	Mock orange

Zingy brights

Sweet pea	Tulip
Common marigold	Perennial phlox
Zinnia	Dahlia
Yarrow	Wallflower
Spider flower	

Jewel colours and autumnal hues

Sunflower

Honeywort

Wild carrot

Masterwort

Sneezeweed

Penstemon

Chocolate cosmos

Ornamental onion

Dahlia

Smoke tree

DRYING AND PRESERVING FLOWERS AND SEEDHEADS

There has been a revival in the fortunes of dried flowers, and today's arrangements are a far cry from the dusty, staid displays of yesteryear. Now, there is an appreciation of the flower in all its stages of growth and senescence. Artists and florists who work with dried flowers see them as a completely different form of the flower to the fresh version, but just as beautiful.

WHAT TO DRY

Drying flowers can be a way to use those stems you didn't get around to cutting and using fresh, or those you left because they weren't good enough. The drying process can mean those imperfections disappear, or transmute into something you can appreciate once dried. You may also like to grow flowers purely for drying.

Most flowers can be dried, providing their stems are not too fleshy (tulips, for example, decay in a wonderfully artistic way but are difficult to dry). Experiment with picking at different stages of growth. There is a certain degree of trial and error involved, and no two years will be the same because of the varying conditions of both the flowers and the weather, but keeping records of what you dried and how will help.

Above Roses dry better in bud than full bloom; experiment to find the best time to cut your flowers so they dry the way you like them.

Left Grasses dry easily and well, and are great to use in autumnal arrangements and wreaths, especially when coloured, like this hare's tail grass.

HOW TO DRY FLOWERS AND SEEDHEADS

First, condition the flowers (see also pp54–5) by stripping off unwanted foliage and standing in water overnight. It may seem nonsensical to put flowers for drying in water, but if they are hydrated and plump before you hang them to dry, they will be stronger and hold their structure better.

The next day, tie them into small bunches with garden twine and hang them upside down. You may need to retie the twine if it becomes loose, as the stems dry and shrink. Hang larger stems individually. You could tie all the bunches to a long branch or old broom handle and suspend that, to make it easier to move the flowers around.

WHERE TO DRY

A good drying room will have a constant, ambient temperature. Fleshier flowers and stems (for example, alliums) need a marginally higher room temperature than the thinner-stemmed flowers such as cornflowers and nigella. It also – unsurprisingly – needs to be dry. The lower the room's humidity, the more successful the drying process will be.

The flowers will keep their colour better if they are dried in the dark, or at least out of direct sunlight. However, you could also experiment with naturally bleaching flowers by hanging them in a very hot and dry place such as a sunny windowsill or greenhouse.

Above Some dried flowers closely resemble their fresh selves, others take on a different kind of beauty.

ARRANGING DRIED FLOWERS AND SEEDHEADS

The muted tones and atmosphere of aging means dried flowers suit autumn and winter displays most, and they can take the place of your fresh flowers as the latter become less available at the season's end, however you may wish to display them all year round. Most dried flowers are best replaced after a year at most.

Dried flowers and seedheads can be arranged in a vase mixed or individually, but also woven into wreaths and garlands. Individual flowers can be separated from their stems and fixed to lengths of cotton to hang as a pretty screen, or glued to a bare branch to mimic cherry blossom in spring (add seedheads such as honesty and bay leaves, too). Allium seedheads can be suspended as huge, natural festive baubles; look at social media for other ideas of using your dried flowers.

PRESSING FLOWERS
....

An alternative way to preserve your cutting garden is by pressing some flowers. You could keep a pressed record of the flowers you grow (a herbarium of your patch), or create artwork using pressed petals, leaves and whole flowers (using dried flowers too adds a 3D aspect and interest).

GOOD FLOWERS FOR DRYING

Amaranthus	Love-in-a-mist
Ammi	Meadowsweet
Astrantia	Monarda
Bay (foliage)	Oregano
Branching larkspur	Rudbeckia
Cornflower	Sea holly
Echinacea	Statice
Feverfew	Strawflower
Geum	Wild carrot
Hydrangea	Yarrow
Lady's mantle	Zinnia
Lavender (also for scented sachets)	

GOOD SEEDHEADS FOR DRYING

Allium	Love-in-a-mist
Cloud grass	Poppy
Foxglove (when still green)	Smokebush
Golden oats grass	Snapdragon
Greater quaking grass	Starflower 'Ping Pong'
Hare's tail grass 'Bunny Tails'	Sweet rocket
Honesty	Switchgrass 'Frosted Explosion'
	Tufted hair grass 'Goldtau'

Dried hydrangea flowers

Dried honesty seedheads

SEED SAVING

Seeds can be one of the biggest outlays for a cut-flower grower, so why not save your own seed? It's extremely satisfying to be able to grow flowers from seeds you grew, either to replace annual crops or, in the long term, to increase your stock of perennials and bulbs.

Above As you're collecting seeds, keep the species separate by using paper cones or something similar, as for these columbine seedheads (see p95).

HOW TO SAVE SEEDS

Letting annuals go to seed will mean they will no longer flower, so stop picking at midsummer to give the seeds time to mature before the winter weather arrives. If you have more than one plant, perhaps only let some go to seed so you can carry on picking flowers from the others, or make two sowings and let the first go to seed but not the second.

Seeds will be ready to gather when they have browned and turned dry and hard, rattling in their seed pods if they have one. Keep checking back until they are ready, or alternatively tie a paper bag over the seedhead, securing it tightly to the stem, so if the seeds fall before you expect you've still caught them in the bag.

Gather seeds on a dry day. Either cut the seedheads from the plant and separate the seeds from their pods and other chaff at a table, or rub the seeds out of their casings over a large bowl while they are still on the plant.

Store your seeds in paper packets, envelopes or bags, securely fastened and labelled with the name of the plant and the date collected. Store in a cool, dry place to sow next year. They may keep after that, but with each passing year it is less likely you will get a good germination rate. However, some seeds, such as hellebores, need sowing straight after collecting in late spring or early summer.

Not all plants will have flowers the same as the ones from which you harvested the seeds: they won't 'come true'. Avoid gathering seeds from F1 hybrid plants in this respect. Other flowers may have cross-bred but still produce healthy plants with pretty flowers – you just have to wait to find out!

Marigold seeds

Fritillaria

GOOD FLOWERS FOR SEED SAVING

Allium	Love-in-a-mist
Amaranthus	Marigold
Cornflower	Nasturtium
Foxglove	Snake's head fritillary
Hellebores	Strawflower
Honesty	Sunflower
Lemon balm	Sweet pea

CHAPTER THREE

Plant Profiles

The magic of planting a tiny seed and watching it grow into a plant, especially one that supplies you with armfuls of flowers, never goes. Bulbs are similarly rewarding and the appearance of their first shoots, and those of your perennial plants, heralds the arrival of a new season. The profiles in this chapter are an introduction to the many beautiful flowers you could grow on your cutting patch, from cottage-garden classics to more unusual blooms. There are so many to choose from, the difficulty will be narrowing down your choices to the available space. Don't forget to make some space for foliage and other plants you can cut, such as grasses, to add variety and seasonal interest to your arrangements.

While every effort has been made to ensure that the varieties of flowers listed in this chapter are widely available, fashion affects horticulture as much as any other industry and inevitably some may fall out of favour or be superseded with better options over time. If you grow varieties you particularly like, saving your own seed is a good way to ensure you'll always be able to sow it again next year.

Sweet pea

Lathyrus odoratus

Sweet peas are the classic cottage-garden cut flower, a staple of summer picking since the 1600s for their incredible scent. Too fleeting to be sold in the shops, they are easy to grow.

GROWING

Sow sweet peas in deep pots (or loo-paper cardboard tubes) in autumn or late winter, and/or sow direct outside in mid-spring. Protect from mice and squirrels and pinch out seedlings.

Support with a wigwam of canes/poles or netting stretched vertically between two posts. Wind string round a wigwam of canes at short intervals to give them enough to hold on to, or loosely tie the young plants onto the canes. Save seed in autumn, then compost the whole plant.

CUTTING

Pick sweet peas regularly in order to keep the plants fresh and producing more flowers. Cut as they are still in bud with as much stalk as possible, with the colour of the petals showing but still closed.

RECOMMENDED VARIETIES

The 'old-fashioned' or heritage choices have the best scent, while the 'Spencer' types of the 1900s have frillier petals and long stems; the 'modern grandiflora' types have large flowers and a fragrance strength depending on the individual variety. Many seed companies offer mixed seeds, which will give you a variety of colours from just one pack, or choose single varieties to make your own mix.

Old-fashioned types: 'King Edward VII', 'Matucana', 'Painted Lady'

Spencer types: 'Beaujolais', 'Eclipse', 'Nimbus'

Modern grandiflora types: 'Cathy', 'Noel Sutton'

Flowering late spring–early autumn

Repeat flowering

Fragrance

Vase life of around 2–3 days

Not good for drying

Height 1.8m (6ft)
Spread 0.3m (1ft)

Cornflower

Centaurea cyanus

Romantic cornflowers add a natural, meadow feel to an arrangement. They are good value cut-and-come-again plants and their narrow, glaucous foliage takes up very little space. The true blue of the species is hard to beat, but there are dark purple, pink and white varieties, too.

GROWING
Sow in autumn for stockier plants, or any time in spring. Pinch out and support plants. Pick and/or deadhead regularly to prolong flowering.

CUTTING
Cut stems as long as possible when the tiny artichoke-like buds are showing some colour. The buds are striking but picked too soon they may not open. To dry, cut and hang the whole plant.

RECOMMENDED VARIETIES
'Black Ball'

'Polka Dot Series'

'Snowman'

Flowering late spring (autumn-sown); early summer to early autumn

Repeat flowering

No fragrance

Vase life of around 7+ days

Good for drying

Height 50cm (20in)
Spread 10cm (4in)

Love-in-a-mist

Nigella damascena

Love-in-a-mist flowers are intricately shaped, with delicate, dissected foliage. The swollen, green and purple striped seedpods can be used fresh in arrangements or dried.

GROWING

Nigella are short-lived plants: sow two or more batches from early spring for a supply through summer (an autumn sowing will give you flowers earlier in the year). To avoid lush foliage at the expense of flowers, don't fertilize, mulch or over-water.

CUTTING

Pick the flowers as the petals start to unfurl and the pods while they are still green. Saved seeds may not come true to type.

RECOMMENDED VARIETIES

N. damascena 'Miss Jekyll'

N. damascena 'Persian Jewels Group Rose'

N. hispanica

N. papillosa 'African Bride'

Flowering late spring (autumn sown); mid–late summer

Repeat flowering

No fragrance

Vase life of around 5–7 days

Good for drying

Height 50cm (20in)
Spread 25cm (10in)

White laceflower

Orlaya grandiflora

Flowering early
summer–early autumn

Repeat flowering

No fragrance

Vase life of around
7–10 days

Not good for drying

Height 60cm (24in)
Spread 30cm (12in)

Orlaya is a large umbelliferous flower, similar to cow parsley, with pure white petals; the petals on the outer florets are longer than those on the interior. Delicate, fern-like foliage sets off the flowers beautifully.

GROWING
Sow under cover in early to mid-spring to plant out in late spring to early summer or sow direct in late spring to early summer; germination can be slow. *Orlaya* will flower around 12 weeks after sowing.

CUTTING
Cut regularly to encourage more flowers. Save seed if you can, as it's relatively expensive to buy.

RECOMMENDED VARIETIES
None widely available.

YOU MAY ALSO LIKE
Annual baby's breath (*Gypsophila elegans*) and the variety 'Covent Garden'

Toothpick plant

Visnaga daucoides syn. *Ammi visnaga*

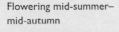

Flowering mid-summer—
mid-autumn

No repeat flowering

No fragrance

Vase life of around
10 days

Good for drying

Height 80cm (32in)
Spread 30cm (12in)

Each domed flower head of the toothpick weed is made of many tiny florets, giving it an airy and delicate appearance. As a filler it adds a frothy, softly romantic and hazy meadow feel to posies and arrangements, but used by itself creates an architectural and sophisticated look.

GROWING

Sow a small batch every two weeks from early spring (under cover) to mid-spring (outdoors) to give you a regular supply through the summer. Needs support.

CUTTING

Cut when around a quarter of the buds on the flower head are fully open.

RECOMMENDED VARIETIES

'Green Mist'

YOU MAY ALSO LIKE

False bishop's weed (*Ammi majus*) and the variety 'Graceland',

Thorow-wax (*Bupleurum rotundifolium*) and the variety 'Griffithii'

Common marigold

Calendula officinalis

Cheery and hardy marigolds can flower from early spring to late autumn depending on the temperature, and will also attract aphid predators such as ladybirds and hoverflies to your patch. Available in many shades of orange and yellow, the petals are also edible.

GROWING

Sow in early spring, or in autumn for an early crop. Regular cutting should produce bushy plants that don't need support. It's easy to save seed, or allow it to self-seed and transplant the seedlings.

CUTTING

The stems need to go straight into water after cutting or they can wilt. Snip off the lower foliage very gently.

RECOMMENDED VARIETIES

'Art Shades' (mixed)

'Indian Prince' (Prince Series)

'Snow Princess'

YOU MAY ALSO LIKE

Chrysanthemum 'Dunnettii'

Chrysanthemum carinatum 'Polar Star' or a proprietary seed mix such as 'Rainbow'

Nasturtium (*Tropaeolum majus*)

Flowering early summer–mid-autumn

Repeat flowering

No fragrance

Vase life of around 7 days

Good for drying

Height 50cm (20in)

Spread 25cm (10in)

Sunflower

Helianthus **species**

The truly giant sunflowers are not generally good subjects for cutting, being so top-heavy in a vase, but there are many smaller and branching varieties in a range of colours. *H. debilis* subsp. *cucumerifolius* will branch more than *H. annuus*, but the latter will produce smaller side flowers after the main flower has been cut. There are pollen-free varieties that won't shed pollen on your table, but these provide no benefit to wildlife.

GROWING

Sow direct in late spring, or earlier in small pots to plant out. Pinch out non-branching types when they are 20cm (8in) tall. Support with individual stakes.

CUTTING

For fresh flowers, cut as the petals start to unfurl (or before, to use as spiky green buds); to dry, cut before the seeds develop.

RECOMMENDED VARIETIES

H. annuus varieties 'Buttercream', 'Red Sun', 'Ruby Eclipse' and 'Valentine'

H. debilis subsp. *cucumerifolius* varieties 'Vanilla Ice' and 'Italian White'

Flowering mid–late summer

No repeat flowering

No fragrance

Vase life of around 7 days

Good for drying

Height 2m (6ft)

Spread 0.6m (2ft)

Flowering mid-summer

No repeat flowering

No fragrance

Vase life of around
1 day (flowers)

Good for drying
(seedhead)

Height 70cm (28in)

Spread 25cm (10in)

Poppy

Papaver **species and varieties**

Although their flowers are as fleeting as they are beautiful, annual poppies have an alternative harvest of their glaucous, rounded seedheads, which are striking on their own, or mixed into fresh or dried arrangements.

GROWING

Sow direct in early autumn or mid-spring, or transplant the grey-leaved, self-sown seedlings. Give the support of stakes or netting.

CUTTING

Enjoy the flowers (and the bees on them) in your patch, then cut the seedheads once the petals have fallen to use fresh or dry. Leave some in the ground to save the seed – it's ready when it is rattling in the pod.

RECOMMENDED VARIETIES

P. somniferum 'Lauren's Grape'

P. rhoeas 'Amazing Grey'

YOU MAY ALSO LIKE

Starflower (*Scabious stellata*) 'Sternkugel' or 'Ping Pong'

Field pennycress (*Thlaspi arvense*)

Fiddleneck

Phaecelia tanacetifolia

Widely used as a green manure (see p49), fiddleneck also makes a wonderful, easy-to-grow cut flower. It is a brilliant, nectar-rich plant to grow for bees and to attract those notable aphid predators, hoverflies. Its intense, lavender-blue flowers are held in intricate, drooping, tail-like clusters (it's also known as the scorpion flower) and the dense foliage will suppress weed seedlings around the plants.

Flowering late spring–early summer

Repeat flowering

No fragrance

Vase life of around 7–10 days

Not good for drying

Height 90cm (3ft)

Spread 30cm (1ft)

GROWING
Sow in early to late spring, direct into the ground. Save seed in autumn, or let it self-seed and transplant the seedlings. Grow through horizontal netting support.

CUTTING
Cut once the colour is fully showing on the lowermost flowers on the 'tail'.

RECOMMENDED VARIETIES
None available.

YOU MAY ALSO LIKE
Honeyweed (*Leonurus sibiricus*)

Honeywort

Cerinthe major

Honeywort is, as its name suggests, extremely popular with pollinating insects, especially bees.

The long, nodding stems have fleshy, glaucous foliage that turns more purple the closer it gets to the tip, where it accents the bell-like, velvety, deep purple flowers.

GROWING
Sow under cover in early spring, or in autumn for an earlier harvest, planting out from late spring. Honeywort self-seeds easily – lift these hardy seedlings and transplant into rows for next year's crop, or save your own seed.

CUTTING
The stems don't travel well out of water and can wilt after cutting – sear to revive them if that happens (see p55). Use honeywort as a foliage plant in spring as well as for its flowers in summer; regular cutting will prolong flowering.

RECOMMENDED VARIETIES

'Purpurascens'

'Kiwi Blue'

Flowering late spring (autumn sowings); early–late summer

Repeat flowering

No fragrance

Vase life of around 7 days

Not good for drying

Height 60cm (24in)

Spread 60cm (24in)

Branching larkspur

Consolida regalis

This annual delphinium brings cottage-garden charm and elegant height to an arrangement with its slender spires of blue, white or pink. *Consolida regalis* has deep, purple-blue flowers, but a mixed packet of seed is an inexpensive way to grow a variety of colours.

GROWING

Keep the seeds in the fridge for better germination rates, although they can still take two months to sprout. Sow under cover in autumn, or early to late spring, and plant out from late spring; support with stakes or netting.

CUTTING

To use fresh, cut when the bottommost flowers on the stem are open; to dry, cut the whole stem once half the buds have opened. The petals (fresh or dried) make excellent confetti.

RECOMMENDED VARIETIES

'Misty Lavender'

'Pink Perfection'

'Exquisite Series'

YOU MAY ALSO LIKE

Clary (*Salvia sclarea*)

Linaria maroccana 'Licilia Red' (Licilia series)

Flowering early summer–early autumn

Repeat flowering

No fragrance

Vase life of around 10 days

Good for drying

Height 1.2m (4ft)

Spread 0.3m (1ft)

Cosmos

Cosmos bipinnatus

Cosmea are a popular and prolific plant for a cutting garden, giving weeks' worth of large, daisy-like flowers well into autumn if temperatures allow. Choose from pastel pinks, pure whites or darker crimsons. Recent breeding has brought in fused (Cupcake series) and different-shaped petals (such as the Pied Piper varieties) to add textural interest, too.

GROWING

Sow under cover in mid-spring and/or outside in late spring after all risk of frost has passed. Pinching out is crucial (see p38), and support by growing through netting.

CUTTING

Cut as the buds begin to unfurl into coloured petals. Deadhead any you miss to keep the plant flowering.

RECOMMENDED VARIETIES

'Purity'

'Rubenza'

'Antiquity'

'Cupcakes Blush' (Cupcakes Series)

'Pied Piper Red'

'Rosetta'

'Velouette'

YOU MAY ALSO LIKE

Annual phlox (*Phlox drummondii*) varieties 'Cherry Caramel', 'Crème Brûlée' and 'Sugar Stars'

Flowering time: Mid-summer–first frost

Repeat flowering

No fragrance

Vase life of around 5–7 days

Not good for drying

Height 1.5m (5ft)

Spread 0.4m (16in)

Tobacco plant

Nicotiana species and varieties

The fragrance of the ornamental varieties of the tobacco plant is delicious and not at all smoky. They add light and airy height to a bouquet, just ensure you choose the taller varieties, not the dwarf, bedding types.

GROWING
Sow under cover from early to late spring. Thin the seedlings, as the seed is so small you'll inevitably sow more than you need. Cover only with the finest layers of compost as they need light to germinate. Plant out once all risk of frost has passed and grow up through netting for support.

CUTTING
Cut the stems once the buds are showing a good amount of colour – you might like to wear gloves against the sticky stems and foliage. Regular cutting will prolong flowering.

RECOMMENDED VARIETIES

N. 'Lime Green'

N. *langsdorfii* 'Bronze Queen' and 'Lemon Tree'

N. *sylvestris*

N. *mutabilis*

Flowering early summer–first frost

Repeat flowering

Fragrance

Vase life of around 5–7 days

Not good for drying

Height 1.5m (5ft)

Spread 0.6m (2ft)

Flowering early summer
(autumn sown); mid-
summer–mid-autumn

Repeat flowering

Fragrance (some varieties)

Vase life of around 7–10 days

Good for drying

Height 75cm (30in)

Spread 35cm (14in)

Snapdragon

Antirrhinum majus

**Snapdragons are short-lived
perennials treated as tender
annuals, as they will flower from
seed in their first year. Their
colourful spires create a cottage-
garden feel in arrangements.**

GROWING

Sow under cover in autumn or late winter
(don't cover the tiny seed), and pinch out when
the seedlings have four sets of leaves. Plant out
after the last frost and grow through netting.

CUTTING

Pick when the lower third of the flowers on the
stem are open. You'll get one main flower spike,
then the side shoots will produce smaller stems
for posies. For dried flowers, pick at the same
time and dry quickly.

RECOMMENDED VARIETIES

'Freesong Apple Blossom' (Freesong Series),
also sold as 'Appleblossom'

'Black Prince'

'Night and Day'

'Monarch Series', mixed, also sold as
'Monarch Mixed'

Blue lace flower

Trachymene coerulea syn.
Didiscus caeruleus

These pretty, delicate flowers form a solid, cushion-like flower head of pale blue-purple atop a long, foliage-free, slightly furry stem. They will flower non-stop for up to three months and are also excellent at attracting useful hoverflies to your cutting patch.

GROWING

Sow under cover in early spring and plant out after the last frost. Germination can be erratic and take up to a month. The plants are low-growing and don't need support, but will sprawl into each other.

CUTTING

Cut the stems once a quarter of the flowers on the head have opened. Regular cutting will encourage further flower production until the first frost.

RECOMMENDED VARIETIES

None widely available.

YOU MAY ALSO LIKE

Annual aster (*Callistephus chinensis*) 'Duchess Series' and 'Lady Coral Lavender' (Lady Coral Series)

Flowering mid-summer–first frost

Repeat flowering

Fragrance (faint)

Vase life of around 7 days

Good for drying

Height 45cm (18in)

Spread 30cm (12in)

Love-lies-bleeding

Amaranthus caudatus

Love-lies-bleeding is a striking and unusual cut flower, good for using with bright colours or lime greens and whites, and for adding an exotic touch to a bouquet. It's best for large displays and tall containers where its bright flower 'tails' or 'tassels' can trail downwards unrestricted.

GROWING

Sow seeds direct in early to late spring and put in horizontal netting supports. The tails can reach up to 1m (3ft) long with plenty of water and access to nutrients.

CUTTING

Cut the flower tails once they are fully developed, with a good section of stem to support them at the desired height in the arrangement. Love-lies-bleeding keeps its colour well when dried, and should be cut for drying when fully mature.

RECOMMENDED VARIETIES

'Viridis'

'Coral Fountain'

'Dreadlocks'

Flowering mid-summer–first frost

No fragrance

Vase life of around 5–7 days

Good for drying

Height 1.2m (4ft)

Spread 1m (3ft)

Spider flower

Cleome hassleriana

The spider flower is a divisive cut flower – its exotic, spiky flowers and stems are wonderful to look at, but for many people the odour outweighs the blooms' visual beauty (it's also known as 'skunk flower' and 'stinking clover').

GROWING
Sow under cover between mid-winter and mid-spring, covering the seeds with a very thin layer of compost. Seedlings can be slow to get started; plant out once all risk of frost is passed. Support by growing through netting.

CUTTING
Cut when they are showing a good amount of colour – beware the thorns. Spider flowers will keep producing flowering stems later into autumn than many other half-hardy, annual, cut flowers.

RECOMMENDED VARIETIES

'Violet Queen'

'White Queen'

'Señorita Rosalita'

Flowering mid-summer–mid-autumn

Repeat flowering

Fragrance (but can be unpleasant)

Vase life of around 5–7 days

Not good for drying

Height 1m (3ft)

Spread 0.3m (1ft)

Zinnia

Zinnia elegans

Bright and bold, zinnias can give a splash of colour to a late summer bouquet, although they can be temperamental plants. Choose taller varieties (not dwarf bedding varieties) for cutting.

GROWING

Sow under cover in mid-spring, potting on if necessary before planting out after the last frost, as they do not like to become rootbound. Alternatively, sow direct in late spring or early summer. Support by growing through netting.

CUTTING

Pick once the petals have opened and remove all leaves from the stem. Dry upright, not hanging upside down.

RECOMMENDED VARIETIES

'Benary's Giant Series'

'Queen Lime Red' (Queen Series)

YOU MAY ALSO LIKE

Black-eyed Susan (*Rudbeckia hirta*)

Everlasting flower (*Xerochysum bracteatum*)

Cosmos (*Cosmos sulphureus*) 'Brightness Mixed' (also sold as 'Bright Lights' mixed)

Flowering late summer–mid-autumn

Repeat flowering

No fragrance

Vase life of around 5–7 days

Good for drying

Height up to 80cm (32in)

Spread up to 40cm (16in)

Mexican paintbrush

Ageratum houstonianum

Each individual floret in the flower head of the Mexican paintbrush plant resembles a tiny, pastel sea anemone. Producing masses of flowers on long stems all summer long and well into autumn, this is an excellent-value plant for any cutting patch.

GROWING
Sow under cover between late winter and mid-spring, then plant out after the last frost. Sow the seeds on the surface of the pots and don't cover them. Mexican paintbrush will tolerate some dappled shade. Support with netting.

CUTTING
Cut stems regularly to prolong flowering; pick when most of the flowers on the head have opened.

RECOMMENDED VARIETIES
'Dondo White'

'Timeless Mixed'

'Blue Horizon'

YOU MAY ALSO LIKE
Sea lavender, also known as statice (*Limonium sinuatum*), which is excellent for drying.

Flowering early summer–first frost

Repeat flowering

No fragrance

Vase life of around 7 days

Not good for drying

Height up to 75cm (30in)

Spread up to 30cm (12in)

Foxglove

Digitalis species and varieties

The tall spires of foxgloves add a wildness to a bouquet, and both the species and the newer varieties have wonderful detailing on the throats of their bell-like flowers.

GROWING

Sow into small pots in mid-summer and plant out in early autumn, ideally in dappled shade. Support with individual stakes or netting the following year.

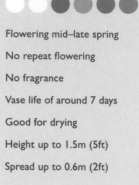

Flowering mid–late spring

No repeat flowering

No fragrance

Vase life of around 7 days

Good for drying

Height up to 1.5m (5ft)

Spread up to 0.6m (2ft)

CUTTING

Cut the main flower stem when half to two-thirds of the flower buds have opened and use fresh or hang to dry. The plant will then produce smaller, secondary, flowering stems.

RECOMMENDED VARIETIES

D. lanata 'Café Crème'

D. purpurea

D. purpurea f. *albiflora*

D. purpurea 'Pam's Choice'

YOU MAY ALSO LIKE

Digitalis purpurea 'Sutton's Apricot', which can be sown as an annual, and the perennial *D. lutea*.

CAUTION

Wear gloves when handling foxgloves, as they can cause light-headedness and potential serious illness, especially in those with heart conditions. The plants can be fatal if ingested.

Honesty

Lunaria annua

Honesty flowers look pretty arranged with some fresh green foliage plants, but leave some or all of the flowers on the plant so you can gather the round, shining, papery seedheads (known as moon pennies) later in the year for winter decorations.

GROWING
Sow in small pots in mid-summer and plant out in autumn for flowers the following year, or transplant self sown seedlings.

CUTTING
Cut when half to two-thirds of the flowers on the stem have opened and use the lower flowering branches in smaller posies. For seedheads, wait until the seedpods are brown and dry, then cut the whole plant. Peel away the brown outer casings to reveal the shimmering disc inside and save the seeds as well.

RECOMMENDED VARIETIES

L. annua var. *albiflora*

YOU MAY ALSO LIKE

Dame's violet, also known as sweet rocket (*Hesperis matronalis*)

Flowering late spring–mid-summer

No repeat flowering

Fragrance (slight)

Vase life of around 7 days

Good for drying (seedpods)

Height up to 80cm (32in)

Spread up to 30cm (12in)

Stocks

Matthiola incana

Stocks can fill a room with their spiced, clove-like scent, and their sweet fragrance is a real highlight of the spring cutting garden. The branching plants produce plenty of stems for cutting before dying back to make room for flowers such as cosmos and dahlias.

GROWING
Sow in early or mid-summer in small pots and plant out in early autumn for flowers the following spring. These small plants will not need support.

CUTTING
Cut the stem on which the first flowers have opened, which will trigger buds on other stems to open too. Change the water regularly to keep them going in the vase.

RECOMMENDED VARIETIES

'Pillow Talk'

'Vintage Mixed' *

'Vintage Brown' *

Flowering mid-spring–early summer

No repeat flowering

Fragrance

Vase life of up to 21 days

Not good for drying

Height up to 35cm (14in)

Spread up to 20cm (8in)

Wild carrot

Daucus carota

The wild carrot is easily one of the best umbel-shaped flowers for cutting, both for the beauty of the dark-purple varieties but also its longevity in the patch and the vase. It's also very forgiving, flowering the following summer even if you forget to sow it until late winter.

Flowering late spring–early autumn

Repeat flowering

No fragrance

Vase life of around 10 days

Good for drying

Height up to 1.2m (4ft)

Spread up to 25cm (10in)

GROWING

Sow direct to the ground any time from mid-autumn to late winter, or start in small pots under cover and plant out in mid-spring. Grow through netting for support.

CUTTING

Pick the flowers once the individual flowers on the flower head start to open. Each plant should produce secondary flower stems after cutting the first ones. Both the flowers and the seedheads can be dried, but don't be tempted to eat the carrot root, which is inedible.

RECOMMENDED VARIETIES

'Dara' (pictured)

'Black Knight'

Iceland poppy

Papaver nudicaule

If the brighter shades of this poppy don't appeal for your spring and early summer posies, try a white variety, as the Iceland poppy is the only way to get that delicate, papery-petalled poppy effect in an arrangement that, unlike other poppies, will last for more than a day once cut.

Flowering late spring–mid-summer

No repeat flowering

No fragrance

Vase life of around 5–7 days

Good for drying

Height up to 30cm (12in)

Spread up to 20cm (8in)

GROWING

Sow in small pots in early to mid-summer and keep the compost moist but not soggy over winter by protecting in a greenhouse, cold frame or similar. Plant out in mid-spring the following year for flowers a few weeks later, ensuring the soil is well-drained. They won't need supports.

CUTTING

Pick as the petals begin to burst from their buds and some colour is visible. The flowers can benefit from searing, but it's generally not necessary. Dry at any stage of their growth.

RECOMMENDED VARIETIES

'Champagne Bubbles Group'

Wallflower

Erysimum cheiri

Wallflowers have a delicious, honey-and-spice scent that easily pervades the whole room, and a choice of rich, jewel-like colours or creamy spring pastels. For the best stems, choose taller varieties not the dwarf bedding packs in the shops.

GROWING
Sow in small pots in early or mid-summer and plant out in a well-drained spot in early autumn for flowers the following spring. The plants won't need support.

CUTTING
Cut the stems when the lower flowers on the flower spike have opened. Smaller side-shoots will develop for a secondary harvest. To dry, wait until at least half the flowers have opened, or dry as a seedhead.

RECOMMENDED VARIETIES

'Ivory White'

'Blood Red'

'Vulcan'

'Fire King'

YOU MAY ALSO LIKE

Sweet Williams (*Dianthus barbatus*) varieties 'Sooty' (Nigrescens Group) and 'Auricula Eyed Mixed' *

Flowering early spring–early summer

No repeat flowering

Fragrance

Vase life of around 5 days

Good for drying

Height up to 40cm (16in)

Spread up to 30cm (12in)

Hellebore

Helleborus **species and varieties**

Hellebores herald the new season with stylish aplomb. To best appreciate their detailed interiors, cut the stems to just a few centimetres (an inch) long and float the flowers face up on the surface of a bowl of water.

GROWING

Plant in autumn, ideally in partial or dappled shade and a rich, moist but well-drained soil. No supports are needed. Cut back dead leaves as required (plants are semi-evergreen).

CUTTING

Cut stems at the base and put them straight in water. The flowers are naturally nodding, and can be lifted in vase arrangements with evergreen foliage and twiggy winter stems.

RECOMMENDED VARIETIES

H. x hybridus varieties 'Harvington Shades of Night', 'Harvington Yellow Speckled' and 'Helen Ballard'

H. odorus

YOU MAY ALSO LIKE

Primrose (*Primula vulgaris*)

Drumstick primulas (*Primula denticulata*)

Polyanthus (*Primula*) Gold-Laced Group

Flowering late winter–early spring

No repeat flowering

Fragrance (some varieties)

Vase life of around 5–7 days

Not good for drying

Height up to 50cm (20in)

Spread up to 50cm (20in)

Masterwort

Astrantia major

The pincushion flowers of masterwort are delicately two-toned in shades of pink, purple or white depending on the variety. They are stalwarts of the cutting patch, producing flowers all season long and foliage that can also be used in arrangements.

Flowering late spring–early autumn

Repeat flowering

No fragrance

Vase life of around 7 days

Good for drying

Height up to 50cm (20in)

Spread up to 50cm (20in)

GROWING
Plant in autumn. Masterwort tolerates most soils and positions, and doesn't require support.

CUTTING
Cut the long stems and foliage at the base of the plant. Pick for drying once the flowers are fully opened.

RECOMMENDED VARIETIES

'Ruby Cloud'

'Midnight Owl'

A. 'Buckland'

A. 'Hadspen Blood'

YOU MAY ALSO LIKE

Water avens (*Geum rivale*)

Macedonian scabious (*Knautia macedonica*)

Columbine (*Aquilegia vulgaris*), varieties such as 'William Guinness' and A. *viridiflora* 'Chocolate Soldier'

Lady's mantle

Alchemilla mollis

Lady's mantle is an ideal filler and an acid-green 'pop' to lift all styles of arrangements. The furry, crinkled leaves are produced around the smaller flower stalks too, like little Elizabethan ruffs.

GROWING

Plant in the autumn, or transplant self-sown seedlings (it will seed about easily and grow more or less anywhere). Lady's mantle tolerates all soils and situations, and doesn't need support. Cut back dead foliage in early winter.

Right Give blowsy, pink peonies a modern feel by pairing them with acid-green lady's mantle.

Flowering early summer–mid-autumn

Repeat flowering

No fragrance

Vase life of around 7 days

Good for drying

Height up to 50cm (20in)

Spread up to 50cm (20in)

CUTTING

Cut the flowers as a long stalk or short spray depending on what you need. Cutting all the flowers in early summer will lead to a second flush in autumn.

RECOMMENDED VARIETIES

A. mollis is best for flowers.

A. conjuncta has pretty, silver-edged leaves but is quite small.

The variety 'Thriller' is more upright.

Peony

Paeonia lactiflora

Opulent peonies are beautiful, frothy and romantic cut flowers. However, their cutting season is short, and they can take some years to bulk up and produce lots of stems, so they are a labour of love.

GROWING

Plant in the autumn. Peonies dislike root disturbance, so try to plant them in a spot you're sure will be their permanent home. Avoid waterlogged soil and support plants with netting to stop them flopping over. Cut back the dead stems in autumn or late winter.

CUTTING

Cut the stems as long as you can and put them straight into water. Cut either when they are still in bud but showing some colour, or just as they open. The flowers can be dried, but need a very warm room for fast drying.

RECOMMENDED VARIETIES

'Sarah Bernhardt'

'Alexander Fleming'

'Duchesse de Nemours'

Flowering late spring–early summer

No repeat flowering

Fragrance

Vase life of around 5–10 days

Not good for drying

Height up to 1m (3ft)

Spread up to 1m (3ft)

Sneezeweed

Helenium varieties

The sunset shades of sneezeweed flowers are bright but not brash, and look especially good in early autumn, when they mirror the tones of the season. If you don't have time or space for sunflowers, sneezeweeds are a great low-maintenance, perennial alternative.

GROWING
Plant in a sunny position in autumn; grow through netting for support. After flowering has finished, leave the stems standing as shelter for insects, then cut back in late winter as the new growth starts.

CUTTING
Cut carefully as the petals begin to unfurl, putting the stems straight into water as they can bruise and wilt relatively easily.

RECOMMENDED VARIETIES
'Moerheim Beauty'

'Sahin's Early Flowerer'

YOU MAY ALSO LIKE
Cone flower (*Echinacea purpurea*)

Cone flower 'Goldsturm' (*Rudbeckia fulgida* var. *sullivantii* 'Goldsturm')

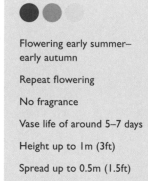

Flowering early summer–early autumn

Repeat flowering

No fragrance

Vase life of around 5–7 days

Height up to 1m (3ft)

Spread up to 0.5m (1.5ft)

Yarrow

Achillea millefolium

Aside from its naturalistic umbels of flowers, produced over a long period in summer, yarrow also has useful frothy, finely cut foliage in late spring and early summer. The flowers can get infested with aphids, but they also attract the aphids' natural predators, hoverflies.

GROWING

Ideally plant in autumn, giving it a position in full sun. Varieties grown from seed should flower the same year. Support the flower stems by growing through netting; cut back the dead foliage in mid- to late winter.

CUTTING

Cut when half of the flowers on the head have opened. Both the flower heads and the seedheads are good specimens for drying.

RECOMMENDED VARIETIES

'New Vintage Violet' *

A. 'Summer Pastels'

A. 'Terracotta'

A. 'Summer Berries' *

YOU MAY ALSO LIKE

Stonecrop 'Herbstfreude Group' (*Hylotelphium* 'Herbstfreude Group', syn. *Sedum*)

American blue vervain (*Verbena hastata*)

Great burnet (*Sanguisorba officinalis*)

Flowering mid–late summer

Repeat flowering

No fragrance

Vase life of around 5–7 days

Good for drying

Height up to 1m (3ft)

Spread up to 1m (3ft)

Penstemon

Penstemon **species and varieties**

Penstemons produce seemingly endless, delicate spires of tubular flowers well into autumn. They are available in a wide range of colours, and the purple-foliaged varieties are useful for adding variety and dark colouring to a bouquet.

GROWING
Plant in a sunny spot in autumn or early spring; protect the roots over winter with a mulch of leaf mould or bark chippings (don't cut back until late winter) and avoid heavy, wet soils. Grow taller varieties through netting for support.

CUTTING
Cut the stems when the lower half of the flowers are open.

RECOMMENDED VARIETIES
'Raven' (Bird Series)

'Osprey' (Bird Series)

P. digitalis 'Dark Towers'

Flowering early summer–late autumn

Repeat flowering

No fragrance

Vase life of around 7 days

Good for drying

Height up to 1m (3ft)

Spread up to 0.5m (1.5ft)

Bergamot

Monarda species and varieties

There are few flowers that look like bergamot, with its whorls of tubular flowers atop each stem, and this low-maintenance perennial is an easy way to inject a more exotic look to your cut flowers. The foliage is wonderfully fragrant, and remains so even when dried.

Flowering mid-summer–early autumn

No repeat flowering

Fragrance (foliage and flower)

Vase life of around 7 days

Good for drying

Height 90cm (3ft)

Spread 30cm (1ft)

GROWING
Plant in a moist but well-drained soil and a sunny position. Water and mulch well, as the plants are susceptible to mildew in dry conditions.

CUTTING
Cut the stems as needed – pick earlier in the season so you are less likely to get mildewed stems.

RECOMMENDED VARIETIES

'Cambridge Scarlet'

Panorama Series

M. citriodora

M. fistulosa (pictured)

Peruvian lily

Alstroemeria varieties

Peruvian lilies are much more productive and better value than lily bulbs, and they last a long time in the vase. Each flower petal is speckled with fascinating, colourful detail.

GROWING

Plant out in mid-spring. They will benefit from netting supports. Peruvian lilies are only hardy to around −5°C (41°F), so in areas with cold, wet winters they are best lifted in autumn (cut back the foliage), planted into pots and stored in a frost-free area until spring.

CUTTING

Peruvian lily stems need pulling, not cutting, or they won't produce more flowers. Firmly hold the base of the flower stem and pull it away from the base of the plant with a slight twist – you can trim the end to a clean cut afterwards.

RECOMMENDED VARIETIES

'Angelina'

'Purple Rain'

'Indian Summer' *

Flowering mid-summer– early autumn

Repeat flowering

No fragrance

Vase life of around 10–14 days

Good for drying

Height up to 90cm (3ft)

Spread up to 30cm (1ft)

Chocolate cosmos

Cosmos atrosanguineus

The velvet-petalled flowers of this cosmos get their name from both their colour and the scent, making it a must-grow for any chocolate lovers. It keeps flowering the more you cut, each bloom borne on long, wiry stems that are ideal for dotting through a bouquet or posy.

GROWING
The plants are not frost-hardy, so lift them and plant in temporary pots in autumn (or grow in pots year-round) and move under protection for winter. Cut back dead foliage in early spring and move outdoors when all risk of frost has passed.

CUTTING
Cut as the petals begin to unfurl from the bud – any earlier and they may not open at all.

RECOMMENDED VARIETIES
Although there are some varieties available, the straight species is the best choice.

Flowering mid-summer– first frost

Repeat flowering

Fragrance

Vase life of around 7 days

Good for drying

Height up to 90cm (3ft)

Spread up to 45cm (1.5ft)

Delphinium

Delphinium species and varieties

If you want to create extremely tall and large arrangements, delphiniums are for you, but otherwise use the shorter and thinner sideshoots, not the main spire. Delphiniums are one of the few truly blue flowers.

GROWING

Plant in autumn in a sunny position. Give each plant its own stake for support. Divide the roots into a few separate clumps and replant every three years to rejuvenate the plants.

CUTTING

Cut when most of the flowers on the spire have opened. Fill the hollow stem with water, trapping it inside with your thumb as you transfer it to the vase, to prolong their vase life. Cutting the main spike will prompt secondary flower shoots to form.

RECOMMENDED VARIETIES

D. 'Crown Jewel'

D. 'Christel'

D. 'Sky Sensation'

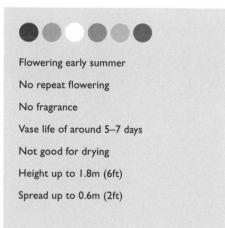

Flowering early summer

No repeat flowering

No fragrance

Vase life of around 5–7 days

Not good for drying

Height up to 1.8m (6ft)

Spread up to 0.6m (2ft)

African lily

Agapanthus varieties

The African lily's loose spheres of trumpet-shaped flowers are especially striking arranged on their own. The classic blue-and-white varieties have now been supplemented with various shades of purple and grey, and also bi-coloured petals.

GROWING
Plant in a sunny spot and very well-drained soil. Cut back the dead foliage in the autumn as it will go slimy over winter otherwise. Plants do not need any supports.

CUTTING
Cut flower stems back to the base when all the flowers are showing colour and put into water straight away. They won't repeat flower.

RECOMMENDED VARIETIES

'Windsor Grey'

'Queen Mum' *

'Purple Cloud'

'Radiant Star'

Flowering mid-summer–early autumn

No repeat flowering

No fragrance

Vase life of around 5–7 days

Not good for drying

Height up to 50cm (20in)

Spread up to 50cm (20in)

Flowering mid–late summer

Repeat flowering

Fragrance

Vase life of around 10 days

Not good for drying

Height up to 1.2m (4ft)

Spread up to 0.6m (2ft)

Perennial phlox

Phlox paniculata

Romantic, soft and scented phlox is a cottage-garden favourite. Choose from soft pastels and whites, or bolder magenta shades; phlox soon fills out an arrangement and has an excellent vase life.

GROWING

Plant in a sunny spot in autumn and divide the clump of roots every three years or so to rejuvenate the plant (and increase your stock). Grow through netting supports and cut back old foliage in late winter.

CUTTING

A good-sized clump will give you plenty of flowers in a single cut and produce more as the season goes on. Pick once most of the buds on the stem have opened, cutting it as long as you need.

RECOMMENDED VARIETIES

'David'

'Rosa Pastell'

'Blue Boy'

'Sweet Summer Fireball' (also known as 'Sweet Summer Red' *

YOU MAY ALSO LIKE

Annual phlox (*Phlox drummondii*) varieties 'Cherry Caramel', 'Crème Brûlée' and 'Sugar Stars'

Flowering mid-summer

No repeat flowering

Fragrance

Vase life of around 10 days

Good for drying

Height up to 90cm (3ft)

Spread up to 60cm (2ft)

Lavender

Lavandula species and varieties

Lavender is perhaps more useful for dried arrangements than fresh, but its narrow, fragrant flower spikes can also add airy height to a posy or hand-tied bouquet.

GROWING
Plant in full sun and a well-drained soil, and only water and feed sparingly. Cut back to where the stems change from soft green-grey to brown when harvesting, or in late summer if you've left some flowers for the bees. Needs no supports.

CUTTING
Cut all the flowers at once and dry what you don't want to use fresh as the harvest window is small. Cut when the bottommost florets on the spike have just opened, which is best for drying; if you're using it all fresh you can wait a little longer.

RECOMMENDED VARIETIES

L. angustifolia

L. x intermedia 'Grosso'

YOU MAY ALSO LIKE

Mugwort for silvery foliage (*Artemisia ludoviciana*)

Michaelmas daisy

Aster species and varieties

Michaelmas daisies help keep a cut-flower patch going into autumn, especially if you are fond of pastel and purple flowers. Cutting them back by a third in late May (the 'Chelsea Chop') will encourage branching (giving you more flowers) but reduce stem length.

GROWING
Plant in autumn; *Aster* prefers a sunny spot and well-drained soil. Grow through netting for support, and leave the dead stems standing over winter for insect shelter, cutting back in early spring.

CUTTING
Cut as the petals begin to unfurl, with as long a stem as you like.

RECOMMENDED VARIETIES
A. amellus 'Rudolph Goethe'

A. × *frikartii* 'Mönch'

YOU MAY ALSO LIKE
Feverfew (*Tanacetum parthenium*)

Flowering late summer–mid-autumn

No repeat flowering

No fragrance

Vase life of around 5–7 days

Good for drying

Height up to 1m (3ft)

Spread up to 0.5m (2ft)

Sea holly

Eryngium species and varieties

The spiny, spiky flowerheads of sea holly come in metallic shades of silver and blue, adding an electric edge to an arrangement. They are also excellent for drying to use on festive wreaths.

GROWING
Plant in autumn. Sea holly prefers hot, sunny and well-drained sites and will not do well where there's soggy winter soil. Plants should not need support.

CUTTING
Cut when the flower heads are fully formed and coloured to use fresh or to dry.

Flowering late summer–early autumn

No repeat flowering

No fragrance

Vase life of around 10 days

Good for drying

Height up to 0.9m (3ft)

Spread up to 0.5m (2ft)

RECOMMENDED VARIETIES

E. giganteum 'Silver Ghost' and 'Miss Willmott's Ghost' (pictured top right)

E. bourgatii

E. planum (pictured top left)

YOU MAY ALSO LIKE

Bladder campion (*Silene vulgaris*)

Globe thistle (*Echinops* species and varieties)

Flowering mid-summer

Foliage spring–late summer

No repeat flowering but foliage regrows

Fragrance (foliage and flowers)

Vase life of around 7 days

Good for drying

Height up to 1.2m (4ft)

Spread indefinite

Mint

Mentha species and varieties

Mint adds a fresh scent to a posy as well as useful bright green foliage. Uncut stems will flower in mid- to late summer, usually small, pale-blue or purple spikes.

GROWING
Plant mint in a pot of multi-purpose, peat-free (or homemade) compost to contain its spreading roots. To rejuvenate it, every other year take it out of the pot, split the roots into thirds and replant just one section back into the pot.

CUTTING
Picking stems will encourage the plant to branch and produce more foliage. Cut low on the stems so secondary branches are also long.

RECOMMENDED VARIETIES
Apple mint (*M. suaveolens*)

Peppermint (*M.* x *piperita*)

Chocolate mint (*M.* x *piperita* f. *citrata* 'Chocolate')

Strawberry mint (*M.* 'Strawberry mint')

YOU MAY ALSO LIKE
Lemon balm (*Melissa officinalis*)

Lemon verbena (*Aloysia citrodora*)

Bay

Laurus nobilis

Bay has a subtle, sweet fragrance and it holds its dark-green leaves strongly upright, giving structure to a bouquet. Its leathery leaves last well out of water, too, making it ideal for wreath-making.

GROWING

Bay can grow into a large tree if allowed, but is easily kept to any manageable size you like by regular cutting to use in arrangements. Plant in a well-drained soil and sunny spot. The evergreen leaves can get scorched (browned) by cold winds, so give it some shelter if possible.

CUTTING

Cut sprigs or stems as needed. Lower leaves you remove can be (dried and) used to infuse into stews and other dishes.

RECOMMENDED VARIETIES

The straight species is the best choice, but the golden-leaved variety 'Aurea' can also be useful in arrangements.

YOU MAY ALSO LIKE

Fennel (*Foeniculum vulgare*) or the variety bronze fennel (*F. vulgare* 'Purpureum')

Rosemary (*Salvia rosmarinus*)

Oregano (*Origanum vulgare*)

Flowering spring

Foliage spring–late summer

No repeat flowering but foliage regrows

Fragrance (foliage)

Vase life of around 10 days

Good for drying (foliage)

Height up to 7.5m (25ft)

Spread up to 7.5m (25ft)

Golden oats grass

Stipa gigantea

Golden oats grass is one of the earliest grasses to produce its flowers and seedheads in summer, which dance beautifully on the end of the stalk. Cut the stalks earlier rather than later in the season – by autumn there's more choice from other grass species and the golden oats can be looking a little tatty.

GROWING
Plant golden oats grasses in a sunny spot and a relatively well-drained soil. They are perennial and evergreen, so only need any dead leaves raking out in late winter or early spring.

CUTTING
Cut the flower stalks from the base as needed.

RECOMMENDED VARIETIES
In a smaller space, try 'Pixie'.

YOU MAY ALSO LIKE
Switch grass 'Frosted Explosion' (*Panicum*)

Cloud grass (*Agrostis nebulosa*)

Korean feather reed grass (*Calamagrostis brachytricha*)

Pheasant's tail grass (*Anemanthele lessoniana*)

Flowering summer to early autumn

No repeat flowering

No fragrance

Vase life of around 10 days

Good for drying

Height up to 2m (6ft)

Spread up to 1m (3ft)

Hare's tail grass

Lagurus ovatus syn.
Lagurus ovatus **'Bunny Tails'**

If you don't have the space or inclination to grow perennial grasses, an annual grass such as hare's tail is a great alternative. The dense, fluffy flower heads really do look like tails and are great in a bouquet, fresh or dried.

GROWING
Station-sow direct (see p36) or sow into small pots in early to mid-spring (they are fully hardy). Don't thin the seedlings and you'll get a more robust clump from which to harvest.

CUTTING
Cut the stems as needed – they become fluffier as they age.

RECOMMENDED VARIETIES
None available.

YOU MAY ALSO LIKE
Greater quaking grass (*Briza maxima*)

Flowering mid-summer–early autumn

No repeat flowering

No fragrance

Vase life of around 10 days

Good for drying

Height 45cm (18in)

Spread 30cm (12in)

Daffodil

Narcissus species and varieties

The arrival of the daffodils on the flower patch signals that the cutting season is truly beginning. There are hundreds of varieties to choose from, flowering from late winter to late spring, in shades from jolly yellow to peaceful white.

GROWING

Plant bulbs in autumn. After cutting the flowers, leave the foliage for six weeks before cutting back to allow the plant to make and store enough energy to flower again next year.

CUTTING

Cut the stems at the base. Daffodils will leak a sticky sap from the cut that can cause dermatitis, so wear gloves or wash it off immediately. Put the cut stems in water, then keep changing the water every 5 minutes until the stems stop oozing sap, after which they can then be arranged.

RECOMMENDED VARIETIES

'Pueblo'

'February Gold'

'Hawera'

'Falconet'

N. poeticus var. *recurvus*

Flowering late winter–late spring

No repeat flowering

Fragrance (some varieties)

Vase life of around 7 days

Not good for drying

Height 30cm (12in)

Spread 10cm (4in)

Hyacinth

Hyacinthus orientalis

Usually seen for sale as potted bulbs, hyacinths actually make a good cut flower. Their heady perfume will easily fill a room, if not the whole house, so you may want to use them sparingly!

GROWING
Plant bulbs in autumn. Leave the foliage to die back before pulling it away.

CUTTING
Cut the flower spikes when half the flowers are open, cutting as near to the base as possible.

RECOMMENDED VARIETIES

'China Pink'

'Delft Blue'

'Peter Stuyvesant'

'Woodstock'

'White Pearl'

'Miss Saigon'

YOU MAY ALSO LIKE

Grape hyacinth (*Muscari armeniacum*)

Flowering early spring

No repeat flowering

Fragrance

Vase life of around 5–7 days

Not good for drying

Height 30cm (12in)

Spread 10cm (4in)

Tulip

Tulipa **varieties**

Tulips are a cut-flower grower's dream: easy to grow and cut, and as simple to arrange as just grouping them in a vase. Choose a palette for your patch (and try a different one next year): rich, bold, jewel-like colours; fresh whites and pretty pastels; or dreamy, romantic shades of apricot and plum.

GROWING

Plant bulbs in late autumn, in raised beds or pots if your soil is heavy or waterlogged. Tulips tend not to perform as well in their subsequent years as their first. If you are leaving the bulbs where you've planted them (see p37), allow 10cm (4in) between bulbs, and cut back the foliage to ground level once it has died down in summer.

CUTTING

Cut the stem as long as you like and remove the lower leaves. The stems of tulips continue to grow after they have been cut, so either trim the ends every couple of days or leave them to sprawl out of the vase.

RECOMMENDED VARIETIES

There is a choice of flower form: the classic goblet shape with rounded or narrowly pointed tips; double tulips that look more like peonies; and 'parrot' tulips with frilly edges to their petals. Some retailers offer collections of varieties themed around a colour palette, or make up your own from single varieties.

'Antraciet'

'Apricot Beauty' (pictured below centre)

'Bellville'

'Black Hero'

'Black Parrot'

'Copper Image'

'Green Star' (pictured below left)

'Purissima'

'Rococo'

'Spring Green'

'Verona'

Flowering early spring

No repeat flowering

Fragrance (rarely)

Vase life of around 10 days

Not good for drying

Height 40cm (16in)

Spread 20cm (8in)

Persian buttercup

Ranunculus asiaticus

The Persian buttercup (often also known as 'ranunculus') is a many-petalled delight, and an excellent early-season substitute for peonies or roses.

GROWING
Plant the tubers in a sunny and sheltered position, and in well-drained soil (a greenhouse is ideal if you have one, grow in pots if your soil is heavy). Give the plants plenty of liquid fertilizer when they are in growth, but after they've died back try to keep the soil around them relatively dry.

CUTTING
Cut stems back to their base.

RECOMMENDED VARIETIES
'Success Venere' *

'Aviv Yellow' (Aviv Series)

'Friandine White Pictotee'

'Hanoi'

'Rhone Pink'

R. 'Butterfly Theseus'

YOU MAY ALSO LIKE
Garden anemone (*Anemone coronaria*) De Caen Group

Flowering late spring–early summer

No repeat flowering

No fragrance

Vase life of around 5–7 days

Not good for drying

Height up to 50cm (20in)

Spread 25cm (10in)

Lily of the valley

Convallaria majalis

Ever popular, lily of the valley has a delicious, evocative and nostalgic scent. Put the flowers in a small vase by themselves where you can appreciate their perfect, miniature, bell-like flowers and fragrance.

GROWING
Plant the bulbs in well-drained soil, or containers of compost mixed with one-third horticultural grit if your ground is heavy. Pull off the dead foliage in summer.

CUTTING
Cut each stem at the base when most of the flowers on the spike are open.

RECOMMENDED VARIETIES
The straight species will likely be the best value per bulb, but the variety 'Bordeaux' has slightly bigger flower spikes, or try *C. majalis* var. *rosea* for pink flowers.

YOU MAY ALSO LIKE
Snowdrops (*Galanthus nivalis*)

Snake's head fritillary (*Fritillaria meleagris*)

CAUTION
All parts of the plant are toxic when ingested.

Flowering late spring

No repeat flowering

Fragrance

Vase life of around 5–7 days

Not good for drying

Height 25cm (10in)

Spread 10cm (4in)

Allium

Allium species and varieties

There is plenty of variety in the drumstick flowers of alliums, from the enormous, firework-style heads of *A. schubertii* to the tight, more ovoid flowers of *A. sphaerocephalon*. Dried, the seedheads look wonderful in a vase by themselves.

GROWING
Plant the bulbs in well-drained soil and a sunny position. Grow the taller varieties through netting. Remove the leaves once they have died back.

CUTTING
Cut once the flower head is fully developed. The onion smell will fade after a day (especially if you change the water), so pick ahead of time if required.

RECOMMENDED VARIETIES

A. sphaerocephalon

A. cowanii

A. hollandicum 'Purple Sensation'

A. cristophii

A. schubertii

A. vineale 'Hair'

Flowering early–mid-summer

No repeat flowering

No fragrance

Vase life of around 7–10 days

Good for drying (seedhead)

Height up to 1m (3ft)

Spread up to 0.4m (1ft)

Lily

Lilium **species and varieties**

Lilies need little introduction, they are a stunning and fragrant cut flower. Grow your own to get a wider range of colours than are available in the shops.

GROWING
Plant bulbs in autumn in a rich, moist, but well-drained soil. Ideally their feet should be in the shade and their heads in the sun. Cut back the rest of the stem once it has died back in autumn.

CUTTING
Cut the stem when the flower buds are fat and just about to open – cut too soon and they may not open at all. Beware the pollen, which can stain surfaces and fabrics.

RECOMMENDED VARIETIES
'Casa Blanca'

'Muscadet'

'Yelloween' *

'Firebolt'

'Stracciatella Event'

L. regale varieties

Flowering early–late-summer

No repeat flowering

Fragrance

Vase life of around 7 10 days

Not good for drying

Height up to 2m (6ft)

Spread up to 0.3m (1ft)

CAUTION
Lily pollen is toxic to pets, especially cats, if ingested so it's advisable to cut off the anthers as soon as the flowers open.

Grassnut

Triteleia laxa

This Californian wildflower is small but perfectly formed for summer posies. Use it as productive and pretty edging for your cut-flower beds if you have mild winters and well-drained soil, but it is only just hardy, so elsewhere it's best planted in pots that can be moved under cover over winter.

GROWING
Plant bulbs in autumn, either direct or in large pots as above, or into small pots you can keep under cover for winter and plant out in spring, lifting them again in the autumn. Remove the foliage once it has died back.

CUTTING
Cut the stems as close to the base as possible.

RECOMMENDED VARIETIES
'Koningin Fabiola' (syn. 'Queen Fabiola')

YOU MAY ALSO LIKE
Guernsey lily (*Nerine* species and varieties)

Flowering early summer

No repeat flowering

No fragrance

Vase life of around 7–10 days

Not good for drying

Height 40cm (16in)

Spread 15cm (6in)

Gladioli

Gladiolus species and varieties

Gladioli are available in a shade to suit every colour palette, from brights to pastels and whites to dusky tones, as well as the smaller, delicate, wild and species gladioli.

GROWING
Plant in well-drained soil and a sunny spot in autumn. Support by growing through netting or individual stakes and cut back dead foliage after flowering.

CUTTING
Pick stems by cutting close to the base when the bottom flowers are showing colour.

RECOMMENDED VARIETIES

G. communis subsp. *byzantinus* (wild gladioli)

G. murielae

G. nanus 'Charm'

G. 'Espresso' *

'Evergreen'

'Bangladesh' *

YOU MAY ALSO LIKE

Monbretia (*Crocosmia* species and varieties)

Flag lily (*Hesperantha coccinea*)

Flowering early–late summer

No repeat flowering

No fragrance

Vase life of around 7–10 days

Not good for drying

Height up to 90cm (3ft)

Spread up to 15cm (6in)

Dahlia

Dahlia varieties

There are more than 1,600 recognized varieties of dahlia in every colour under the sun (except blue), and flower styles from simple daisies to elaborate pom-poms and spiky starbursts. Many have sultry, dark-purple foliage. Additionally, they will produce masses of flowers from late summer to early autumn, making them an ideal cut flower. Not all have a good vase life though, and for the most reliable blooms once cut, choose from the 'Karma' range.

Flowering mid-summer–first frost

Repeat flowering

No fragrance

Vase life of around 5–7 days

Good for drying

Height up to 1.5m (5ft)

Spread up to 0.6m (2ft)

GROWING

Plant tubers in pots under cover in spring (check for rotten parts), then plant out after the last frost into soil that has had plenty of organic matter added to it. Pinch out the tips when the plants are around 40cm (16in) tall. Grow through netting for support. Deadhead any blooms not cut to prolong flowering. Cut back to the ground after the first frost and unearth the tubers, store upside down in a slatted tray or similar to dry off, then wrap in newspaper (labelled) and keep in a cool, dry place over winter.

CUTTING

Cut back to the lowest branching point possible when the bud is showing some colour. For dried flowers, cut open flowers and dry as quickly as possible in a warm room.

RECOMMENDED VARIETIES

'Sam Hopkins'	'Veronne's Obsidian'
'Crème de Cassis'	'Labyrinth'
'Karma Choc'	'White Star'
'Crème de Cognac'	'Brown Sugar'
'Café au Lait Royal'	'Bishop' series

Rose

Rosa species and varieties

Is there a flower more loaded with romance, history and meaning than the rose? Most commercially grown roses have been bred for longevity, and these varieties have lost their scent and blowsy garden charm along the way. Home-grown blooms may not last as long in the vase, but they are worth every penny of their investment for the few days of pleasure they give. If you don't have much ground space, consider growing a climbing rose against a wall or fence instead.

GROWING

Roses like a sunny position and a rich, moist, but well-drained soil. Regular mulching and an occasional liquid feed through the growing season will keep them happy. Prune them in winter while the plant is dormant to remove dead stems and keep the plant open so air can circulate. Roses won't need supports unless you are training them against a wall, in which case tie them to a trellis, or strong wires fixed horizontally to the wall at 45cm (18in) intervals.

CUTTING

Cut roses as the buds begin to unfurl (to use fresh or dry), taking as much stem as possible. Deadhead any you don't cut to prolong flowering.

RECOMMENDED VARIETIES

'A Shropshire Lad'

'Fritz Nobis'

'Madame Hardy'

'Prosperity'

'Buff Beauty'

'Madame Alfred Carrière'

'Compassion'

'Munstead Wood' *

'Gertrude Jekyll' *

'Tuscany Superb'

Flowering early summer–early autumn

Repeat flowering (some species and varieties)

Fragrance (some species and varieties)

Vase life of around 5–7 days

Good for drying

Height up to 1.5m (5ft)

Spread up to 1m (3ft)

Cherry

Prunus **species and varieties**

A single branch of cherry blossom in a large vase is an easy yet spectacular springtime display. There are many small and narrow varieties available if you've only a small space.

GROWING
Plant trees in a sunny spot and moist but well-drained soil. Cutting a few branches for displays each year should be all the pruning they need, but let the tree establish for a few years first.

CUTTING
Cut to where the branch forks, or back to the trunk when the buds are coloured and fat but not open. Only take a branch or two each year. Split the end (see p53) before putting into water.

RECOMMENDED VARIETIES
Any ornamental cherry trees are suitable for cutting; avoid cutting fruiting trees as you'll get less fruit.

YOU MAY ALSO LIKE
Guelder rose (*Viburnum opulus*)

Crab apple (*Malus* species and varieties)

Blackthorn (*Prunus spinosa*)

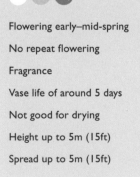

Flowering early–mid-spring

No repeat flowering

Fragrance

Vase life of around 5 days

Not good for drying

Height up to 5m (15ft)

Spread up to 5m (15ft)

Winter-flowering honeysuckle

Lonicera fragrantissima

Ideal for planting in an out-of-the-way place, winter-flowering honeysuckle can be cut for foliage in the summer, but it is most spectacular in late winter, when its branches burst into a wonderfully fragrant display of delicate, yellow-white blossom.

GROWING

Plant in autumn; it will grow in most soils and situations including partial shade. Regular cutting for the vase should be all the pruning it needs.

Flowering late winter

No repeat flowering

Fragrance

Vase life of around 5 days

Not good for drying

Height up to 2m (6ft)

Spread up to 2m (6ft)

CUTTING

Cut branches when the flower buds are almost open.

RECOMMENDED VARIETIES

The straight species is the best choice, or try the other form of winter-flowering honeysuckle, *L. × purpusii*, especially its variety 'Winter Beauty'.

YOU MAY ALSO LIKE

Honeysuckle *Lonicera × purpusii* 'Winter Beauty'

Arrowwood *Viburnum × bodnantense* 'Dawn' or 'Charles Lamont'

Yellow wintersweet *Chimonanthus praecox*

Forsythia *Forsythia × intermedia*

Hydrangea

Hydrangea species and varieties

Hydrangea bushes may take up a fair amount of space in your cutting patch, but their flowers (and foliage) are excellent value. They are large, so they give structure to a bouquet. Some varieties change colour through the season, and they can be dried as flowers or seedheads.

Flowering mid-summer–early autumn

No repeat flowering

No fragrance

Vase life of around 7 days

Good for drying

Height up to 2.5m (8ft)

Spread up to 2.5m (8ft)

GROWING
Plant in autumn in a moist but well-drained soil. Hydrangea will tolerate some partial or dappled shade. They will need no support, and regular cutting should be all the pruning they need.

CUTTING
For fresh flowers, cut when most of the flowers on the head have opened. To dry, cut the fully opened flower heads or leave to turn to seedheads and then dry them.

RECOMMENDED VARIETIES

H. paniculata 'Limelight' *

H. paniculata 'Wim's Red' *

H. paniculata 'Vanilla Fraise' (pictured below)

H. arborescens 'Annabelle'

Mock orange

Philadelphus species and varieties

**The deliciously scented flowers
of mock orange are a wonderful
addition to a summer bouquet,
or just put a few branches in a vase
on their own to better appreciate
their simple, pure-white beauty.**

GROWING

Plant mock orange shrubs in autumn in a
rich, moist, but well-drained soil for the
best flowering and growth. Regular cutting
of flowered branches will be all the pruning
it needs, but remove any dead branches
if necessary.

CUTTING

Cut flowering branches as needed, which
will promote new flowering growth the
following year. Prioritize crossing or inward-
growing branches as that will help the
shrub's overall health, too.

RECOMMENDED VARIETIES

'Belle Etoile'

'Manteau d'Hermine'

Lilac (*Syringa* species and varieties)

Flowering early summer

No repeat flowering

Fragrance

Vase life of around 5 days

Not good for drying

Height up to 2m (6ft)

Spread up to 2m (6ft)

Cider gum

Eucalyptus gunnii

Although they can grow to large trees, regular cutting of the cider gum's foliage will both keep the plants to a manageable size and promote the growth of the rounded, juvenile foliage over that of the elongated, older leaves.

GROWING
Plant in well-drained soil in full sun. If cutting for foliage has not sufficiently restricted the plant's size, it can be pruned back hard in early spring.

CUTTING
Cut branches as needed; they are evergreen and can be used year-round.

RECOMMENDED VARIETIES
'Blue Ice'

'Silver Drop'

YOU MAY ALSO LIKE
Spindle (*Euonymus*) species

Laurustinus (*Viburnum tinus*) and the variety 'Gwenllian'

Christmas box (*Sarcococca confusa*)

Holly (*Ilex*) species

Ivy (*Hedera*) species

Foliage all year

No repeat flowering but foliage regrows

Fragrance (foliage)

Vase life of around 10 days

Not good for drying

Height up to 12m (39ft)

Spread up to 8m (26ft)

Smoke tree

Cotinus coggygria

The matt-purple foliage of the smoke tree is extremely useful as a foil for the flowers in arrangements from spring to autumn, and the large plumes of summer flowers can be used, too. It's deciduous, so use a *Pittosporum*, below, for evergreen/winter purple foliage.

GROWING

The smoke tree will grow in sun or partial shade and most soils; plant in autumn. It will not need supports.

CUTTING

Cut and put directly into water as the branches need to be well-conditioned before arranging.

RECOMMENDED VARIETIES

'Royal Purple'

'Young Lady' *

YOU MAY ALSO LIKE

Tawhiwhi (*Pittosporum tenuifolium*) 'Purpureum' or 'Tom Thumb'

Ninebark *Physocarpus opulifolius* 'Red Baron'

Foliage spring–autumn

No repeat flowering but foliage regrows

No fragrance

Vase life of around 5–7 days

Not good for drying

Height up to 4m (12ft)

Spread up to 4m (12ft)

Flowering late spring–late summer

Repeat flowering

Fragrance

Vase life of around 5–7 days

Not good for drying

Height up to 8m (24ft)

Spread up to 2m (6ft)

Honeysuckle

Lonicera species

Honeysuckle is wonderful for adding scent and a wild, hedgerow beauty to a bouquet, as it twines and trails from the vase. It is quite vigorous and flowers over a long period, so you can cut it to your heart's content.

GROWING

Plant at the base of a strong wall or fence with adequate trellis or wire supports on which to train and tie the stems. Keep well-watered at the base in hot weather, as it can be prone to mildew.

CUTTING

Cut stems as long as you need as the buds are about to open.

RECOMMENDED VARIETIES

Japanese honeysuckle (*Lonicera japonica*)

Honeysuckle 'Graham Thomas' (*L. periclymenum* 'Graham Thomas')

YOU MAY ALSO LIKE

Necklace vine (*Muehlenbeckia complexa*)

Clematis

Clematis species and varieties

There are so many different types of clematis, from vigorous, evergreen species to compact border specimens, and they can be useful additions to a cut-flower patch for their pretty flowers and their fluffy seedheads (*C. tangutica* types, known as 'old man's beard', are the best for seedheads).

Flowering early–late summer; late winter

No repeat flowering

Fragrance (some varieties)

Vase life of around 5 days

Not good for drying

Height up to 3m (9ft)

Spread up to 1m (3ft)

GROWING
Clematis will do best in a rich, moist, but well-drained soil, with its growth in the sun. Plant in autumn to grow up a wall, arch or wigwam of canes, depending on its ultimate size.

CUTTING
Cut stems when they are still in bud and they'll open in a warm room, or wait until the buds are starting to unfurl. Condition as for woody stems (see p53).

RECOMMENDED VARIETIES

C. armandii

C. 'Bill Mackenzie'

C. 'Alionushka'

C. 'Justa'

Dogwood

Cornus species and varieties

Dogwoods supply some of the best coloured stems for winter displays. Cutting them back each year for the stems mean they take up relatively little space for a shrub, so consider planting a few different colours that you can weave into multicoloured wreaths.

GROWING
Plant in a rich, moist, but well-drained soil in sun or partial shade; feed well with mulch each year so they can sprout new stems ready for the following winter.

CUTTING
Cut the stems back to the same point each year, whether that's the ground or a short 'leg' you've allowed to grow up. Stems don't need to stand in water if they are being used by themselves.

RECOMMENDED VARIETIES

C. alba 'Sibirica'

C. sanguinea 'Midwinter Fire'

YOU MAY ALSO LIKE

Willow (*Salix*) species and varieties

Corkscrew hazel (*Corylus avellana* 'Contorta')

Stems autumn–winter

Stems will regrow within a year

No fragrance

Vase life of around 14 days

Not good for drying

Height up to 2m (6ft)

Spread up to 2m (6ft)

Goat willow

Salix caprea

Left unchecked, goat willow (more widely known as pussy willow) will quickly grow into a large tree, but it can be cut back to the ground each year for its winter stems covered in fluffy buds. Leave some on the tree to feed the bees though, as they are rich in pollen when they open.

GROWING
Plant in a rich, moist, but well-drained soil in a sunny spot. Any branches you leave on for the bees can be cut back in late spring. Cut back to the ground or the same point on a short trunk/'leg' each year.

CUTTING
Cut as you would for pruning, when the buds are grey and fluffy.

RECOMMENDED VARIETIES
None widely available.

YOU MAY ALSO LIKE

Larch (*Larix* species), in the winter for its branches still holding small cones

Hawthorn (*Crataegus* species), in early winter for bare stems with red berries

Budding stems late winter–early spring

Stems will regrow within a year

No fragrance

Vase life of around 14 days

Not good for drying

Height up to 2m (6ft)

Spread up to 2m (6ft)

GLOSSARY

ANNUAL
A plant that grows from a seed, flowers, sets seed and dies within a single year.

APHID
Small, green, black, yellow or red bugs that feed on the sap of young plant shoots and leaves.

BIENNIAL
A plant that is sown in summer and will grow leaves, but will not flower until the following spring or summer, after which it sets seed and dies.

BULB
A plant that grows foliage and flowers each year from an underground fleshy root that remains in the soil.

CHELSEA CHOP
A gardening cutting-back practice usually done in the third week of May to coincide with the RHS Chelsea Flower Show. The top third of the foliage of late-summer flowering plants is cut off to encourage branching, stop plants flopping and delay flowering until later in the season.

CORM
A plant very similar to a bulb, but the fleshy root is not bulbous in shape.

DIRECT SOWING
Sowing seeds straight into the soil, raised bed or large container where they are to grow to maturity.

GREEN MANURE
(also called a cover crop). Plants sown into soil that won't be used for a while, often over winter, to prevent soil erosion and nutrient loss, and/or to add nutrients to the soil.

GREY WATER
Washing-up or bath water.

HALF-HARDY
(annual or perennial) A plant whose foliage and flowers will not survive a frost.

HARDENING OFF

The process of gradually acclimatizing plants raised under cover to the cooler conditions outside.

HARDY ANNUAL

Annual plants that will tolerate cold weather and a frost.

HERBACEOUS PERENNIAL

A plant whose foliage and flowers die back in autumn, but shoot anew from the roots in spring.

MILDEW

A plant disease that causes white blotches on the leaves, which eventually die. Usually infects plants whose roots are too dry, especially if the air around the foliage is humid.

MULCH

A layer of organic matter such as compost, leaf mould or bark chippings (or inorganic matter such as gravel), spread over a flowerbed. Functions of an organic mulch include improving soil fertility and structure, moisture retention and weed suppression.

PERENNIALS

Plants that grow year after year, including herbaceous perennials, shrubs and trees.

pH

A measure of the acidity or (its opposite) alkalinity of the soil. Most plants grow best in a soil that is neither too acid (a pH of lower than 5.5) or too alkaline (a pH of higher than 8). Regularly adding horse manure as a mulch can make a soil less acid, but making soil more acid is more difficult even in the long term.

POTTING ON

Planting a potted seedling or young plant into a larger pot.

ROOT FLARE

The point at which the plant's trunk or shoots turn into roots. This should be at soil level when planting.

STATION SOWING

Making individual holes along a row in the ground, spaced accordingly, and dropping in (usually two) seeds before covering them over (as opposed to sprinkling seeds along a row and thinning later).

THINNING SEEDLINGS

Selecting the strongest of the seedlings and removing the rest.

TUBER

A fleshy root similar to a bulb, such as with dahlias.

FURTHER RESOURCES

BOOKS

Cut Flower Growing: A Beginner's Guide to Planning and Styling Cut Flowers, No Matter Your Space by Marianne Slater (Hardie Grant Books, 2022)

Everlastings: How to grow, harvest and create with dried flowers by Bex Partridge (Hardie Grant Books, 2020)

Floret Farm's Cut Flower Garden: Grow, Harvest and Arrange Stunning Seasonal Blooms by Erin Benzakein (Chronicle Books, 2017)

Flower Gardening for Beginners: A Guide to Growing and Maintaining a Cut-Flower Garden by Amy Barene (Rockridge Press, 2022)

Flowers Forever: Celebrate the Beauty of Dried Flowers with Stunning Floral Art by Bex Partridge (Hardie Grant Books, 2022)

Growing Flowers: Everything You Need to Know About Planting, Tending, Harvesting and Arranging Beautiful Blooms by Niki Irving (Mango, 2021)

RHS The Little Book of Wild Gardening by Holly Farrell (Mitchell Beazley, 2022)

RHS How to Grow Plants from Seed by Sophie Collins & Melissa Mabbitt (Mitchell Beazley, 2021)

USEFUL WEBSITES

Royal Horticultural Society (RHS)
rhs.org.uk
Make the RHS website your first port of call – it offers a mass of free information about plants and how to grow them, and dozens of sources where you can buy plants, both in person and online.

Flowers from the Farm
flowersfromthefarm.co.uk
In the UK, this online directory is a good source of information on local flower growers. Find one of your local growers and visit on an open day, or a pick-your-own day, to see which flowers grow well in your area's soil and climate.

NOTES

Buying plants
All the plants in this book are widely available. Avoid buying seeds or plants from abroad to avoid inadvertently importing unknown diseases or pests that could become a problem in your local ecosystems. Always buy seeds and plants from reputable nurseries or growers, and check them thoroughly for signs of diseases and pests.

Selling plants
Note that if you are thinking of selling some of your flowers, it's illegal to sell those where the breeder has registered their rights over it (a little like copyright). Most flowers in Chapter 3 have no restrictions on them, but any that have are marked with an asterix. They will also be listed in the RHS Plant Finder as "subject to Plant Breeders' Rights".

Plant names
The plants in Chapter 3 are referred to by their common names along with their botanical Latin names. The Latin name usually consists of two parts, the genus and species; where the genus is repeated in the text, it is shortened to its first letter. For example, love-in-a-mist's Latin name *Nigella damascena* is shortened to *N. damascena*. Varieties follow these names in inverted commas, such as *N. damascena* 'Miss Jekyll', but sometimes a plant isn't a particular species, and so has just the genus and variety, such as *N.* 'Midnight Blue'.

INDEX

CREDITS

Alamy 18 © RM Floral • 19 © Bailey-Cooper Photography • 37t © Deborah Vernon • 38 © Tim Gainey • 39 © Susan Kennedy • 40 © Kay Roxby • 41 © Matthew Taylor • 49 © Deborah Vernon • 78 © amomentintime • 89 © Zena Elea • 92 © Garden Photo World • 102 © Ros Crosland • 112 © Clare Gainey • 116l © Clare Gainey • 122 © Tamara Kulikova

Dreamstime 79 © Iva Vagnerova • 95 © Elenarostunova • 104 © Andersastphoto • 107 © Jurgen Kleykamp • 136 © Reinout Van Wagtendonk

Freepik.com 55 © cookie_studio

GAP Photos 84 © Stocks and Green

Getty Images 5tr © Deb Perry • 13 © Jacky Parker Photography • 14 © Ivonne Wierink • 15 © Anastasia Ness • 34 © Aleksandr Zubkov • 46l © Cavan Images • 52 © Betsie Van der Meer • 56 © Westend61 • 59b © Meghann Grah/EyeEm • 68r © Ken Leslie • 77 © Jacky Parker Photography • 103 © lacaosa • 114 © Ekaterina Dorokhova/EyeEm • 129 © Maria Mosolova

iStock 42 © wernerimages • 59tr © capecodphoto • 71 © simonbradfield • 82 © np-e07 • 87 © fotolinchen

living4media 59tl © Hippel, Regina

PIXTA 58t © Limesoda

pxfuel.com 96–97

Shutterstock 5tl © Alex Manders • 8t © Andrew Fletcher • 10 © goodmoments • 22 © MarCaLo • 24 © mcajan • 26t © Andy Hoech • 26b © Gouget Camille • 27 © t.sableaux • 28tl © Bozena Fulawka • 28bl © ElephantCastle • 28bcl © photka • 28bcr © Stock Up • 28br © carroteater • 29tl © New Africa • 29tr © A.Krotov • 29cl © WITSALUN • 29ccl © Ortis •

29 ccr © Marina Lohrbach • 29cr © max dallocco • 29bl © Angorius • 29br © Amberside • 30 © Ground Picture • 31 © Michael Lukhanin • 32l © Maxal Tamor • 32tr © Alesikka • 32b © Vilor • 33tr © moo_mon • 33cl © HalinaPalina • 33br © InfoFlowersPlants • 35 © Skeronov • 36 © Agatha Koroglu • 37 © Evgenia Tuzinska • 43 © imm49 • 44 © Deyan Georgiev • 45 © David Prahl • 46–47 © Mariana Serdynska • 47r © Oleksandr Khmelevskyi • 51tl © Lucy Left • 51tr © Anne Coatesy • 51b © Andy119 • 53 © FotoHelin • 54 © laszlo • 57 © Rawpixel.com • 60 © Shokhina • 61l © Pirat Pirat • 61r © New Africa • 62 © Mira Panacek • 63l © Jan J. Photography • 63r © Tamara Kulikova • 64 © VH-studio • 65l © Keith Hider • 65r © Nataly Studio • 68l © Lacey Dent • 69 © photographyfirm • 70 © KPG-Payless • 72 © H.Tanaka • 73 © Kit Leong • 74 © yuris • 75 © MaskaRad • 76 © Mami Nozaki • 80 © Maliutina Anna • 81 © Totokzww • 83 © JackieTeh • 85 © Somchai Siriwanarangson • 86 © Lori Knapper • 91 © Ole Schoener • 93 © GOR Photo • 94 © Fotimageon • 98 © Natali Nedzvetckaia • 99 © kukuruxa • 100 © Nancy J. Ondra • 101 © Jerrold James Griffith • 105 © Kanitarty69 • 106 © Razumhelen • 108 © Auhustsinovich • 109l © Salamanca1218 • 109r © Fabian Junge • 110 © Jiri Hera • 111 © Burhan Oral GUDU • 113 IamTK • 114 © Sergey V Kalyakin • 116–117 © Alienor Llona Bonnard • 118 © AllUneed • 119 © Iryna Tsiareshka • 120 © Look Studio • 121 © Nazzu • 124 © Bogdan Sonjachnyj • 125t © Craig Russell • 128 © SaskiaAcht • 130l © Pcholik • 130r © Natalia Van Doninck • 131 © Victoria P. • 132 © Totokzww • 133 © Max_555 • 134 © olenaa • 135 © bonilook • 137 © New Africa • 138 © RAJU SONI

Unsplash 5bl © Zeynep Elif Ozdemir • 5br © Brigitte Tohm • 6 © Larisa Birta • 9b © Alina Karpenko • 16 © Charlota Blunarova • 17 © JulieK2 • 23 © Calaful Prints • 48 © Yoksel Zok • 58b © Sammi • 66 © Elena Popova • 88 © Cindy Williams Moore • 90 © Felicity Mikellides • 117r © Brigitte Tohm • 123 © Evelien Van Den Bink • 125c © Lynnelle Cleveland • 125b © Annie Spratt • 127tl © Rikonavt • 127tr © Ankit Choudhary • 127b © Joyous Chan • 140–141 © Dagmara Dombrovska • 143 © Christie Kim